MOSES

MOSES

GOD'S MAN
FOR CHALLENGING TIMES

Roger Ellsworth

 EVANGELICAL PRESS

EVANGELICAL PRESS
Faverdale North Industrial Estate, Darlington, DL3 0PH
England

Evangelical Press USA
P.O. Box 84, Auburn, MA 01501, USA

e-mail: sales@evangelicalpress.org

web: http://www.evangelicalpress.org

First published 2005

British Library Cataloguing in Publication Data available

ISBN 0 85234 586 0

Printed in the United States of America

In honour of my dear friends:

Bob and Jody Fuson

CONTENTS

1 | The world into which Moses was born

Exodus 1

Three men tower above all the others in the Old Testament: Abraham, Moses, and David. Of these three, Moses may be regarded as the greatest. As Israel's deliverer, leader and law-giver, he moulded a multitude of slaves into a nation.

These are well-known historical details, but why should anyone who is not interested in history, concern himself with the life of Moses? Here are some answers:

> • The life of Moses is recorded in the Bible, which is the Word of God. Every child of God has an interest in studying the Word of God, and Moses occupies a significant portion of God's Word. He was the author of the first five books of the Bible, and he is the dominant figure in four of those books. He is mentioned at least 47 times in the New Testament.

> • Every child of God is interested in God's plan of redemption, and with Moses the Lord moved this plan forward in a very significant way.

> • The life of Moses presents us with difficulties and challenges much like those we are facing today. As we study his life, we shall find comfort in knowing that our God is as sufficient for us as he was for Moses.

With these things in mind, we set out to study the life of Moses. But the proper place to begin is not with Moses himself but rather with the world into which he was born.

The history of Israel going to Egypt

The book of Exodus opens with the people of Israel being in bondage in Egypt. We remember how the Israelites came to be in Egypt. It happened when Joseph, one of the twelve sons of Jacob, rose to a position in Egypt second only to Pharaoh himself (Gen. 41:37-43).

Early in Joseph's tenure a severe famine decimated the land in which his people, the Israelites, had been dwelling, that is, the land of Canaan. To preserve his people from the famine, Joseph moved his father and all his brothers and their children to the land of Egypt (Gen. 45:9-10).

All went well with the Israelites in Egypt until Joseph died. Then 'there arose a new king over Egypt, who did not know Joseph' (v.8).

This should not be taken to mean that this new ruler had never heard of Joseph but rather that he had no real knowledge of him. John Currid writes: 'It is unlikely that this new king would have been the immediate successor anyway since the Hebrews were in Egypt for over four centuries…It is also possible that the new pharaoh may have been a foreign invader who knew nothing of Joseph.'[1]

The Israelites had grown to a very large number when this new king came on the scene, and he, terrified by the prospect of them becoming dominant, said to his people: 'Look, the people of the children of Israel are more and mightier than we; come, let us deal wisely with them, lest they multiply, and it happen, in the event of war, that they also join our enemies and fight against us, and so go up out of the land" (vv.9-10).

At that point, the Egyptians made the Israelites their slaves (v.11).

The history behind the history

We are wrong to look upon the Egyptians' enslavement of the Israelites as nothing more than a political strategy. There was something else at work here.

Christians know that there are two levels of reality at work in history. Behind human events a spiritual drama is being worked out.

This spiritual drama is clearly set out in Genesis 3:15:

And I will put enmity
Between you and the woman,
And between your seed and her Seed.
He shall bruise your head,
And you shall bruise his heel.

We are familiar with these words. They were spoken in the Garden of Eden by God to Satan after the latter had led Adam and Eve (and the whole human race) into sin.

With these words, the Lord God promised that he would send a Saviour for sinners (the Seed of the woman - Gal. 4:4).

These words also indicate that the human race would from that point be divided into two parts. One part, those who belong to Satan, would oppose and seek to destroy the other part, that is, those who belong to Christ.

From that time forward, the truth of Genesis 3:15 has been worked out in human history. The first example of this is found in the first two sons of Adam and Eve. The one who belonged to Satan – Cain – hated and killed the one who belonged to the Lord – Abel.

The rest of the book of Genesis reflects the opposition of Satan and his people toward the Lord and his people.

Now we are in a position to understand the opening chapter of Exodus. God had designated Israel as the nation into which the Messiah would be born. It is no surprise, then, that Satan would seek to destroy the Israelites.

The first chapter of Exodus presents three of Satan's attacks against Israel:

+ the command to enslave the Israelites (vv.9-11)
+ the command to the midwives to kill male Israelite babies (vv.15-16)
+ the command to all Egyptians to throw all male Israelite babies into the river (v.22).

The hope in the history

All of these details have a lot more to do with us than most people – even Christians – seem to realise. On the basis of what we have noticed, we can say that Satan has not changed. He is still alive, and he still actively opposes God and the people of God. We see that opposition in the outright persecution of Christian people in many nations.

In other nations the persecution, while not overt, is nevertheless underway as Christians are increasingly held up as objects of ridicule and scorn. If any other minority group were treated as Christians are, there would be outrage. But often those who regard themselves as champions of minority rights find that they cannot muster much indignation about the persecution of Christians. And, irony of ironies, these supposed champions are sometimes in the vanguard of it.

This is astonishingly ironic. Christianity has contributed much to the nations of the world, even as Joseph contributed much to Egypt. But we are living in a different time. A king has risen who knows not Joseph. In other words, a time has arrived in which many do not understand and appreciate the good that Christianity has done.

We can go even further. As Pharaoh feared the Israelites, so many today openly express their fear of evangelical Christians. One poll asked respondents to choose the type of people they would least like to have as neighbours. Bible believing Christians topped the list!

We live in times in which the dark storm clouds of opposition and hatred are increasingly gathering over the people of God. The stage is being set for anti-Christ. The times are so dark and troubling that many Christians find themselves disheartened and discouraged.

But the opening chapters of Exodus yield another truth, namely, the God of the Israelites and Moses, is also alive and well. With all he did to wipe the Israelites off the face of the earth, Satan failed. He failed because God saw to it. God would not allow his people to be destroyed and the promise of the Messiah to be negated. God raised up Moses, delivered the people of Israel from their bondage, constituted them into a nation, preserved them in their wilderness wanderings and finally established them in the land of Canaan.

Let the devil rage and gather his forces as a flood. The same God who preserved his cause and his people in ancient times is committed to preserving his cause today. We know this from no less an authority than the Lord Jesus Christ himself who said: 'I will build My church, and the gates of Hades shall not prevail against it' (Matt. 16:18).

2 | Why does God allow his people to suffer?

Exodus 1:13-14; 2:23-25; 3:7-8

The words used in these verses to describe Israel's condition in Egypt are arresting and gripping: 'bitter' (1:13), 'rigor' (1:13-14), 'hard bondage' (1:14), 'oppression' (3:7).

There is no way these words can be toned down. The people of Israel were living very difficult lives in Egypt. Life was hard. The hours were long. The workload was heavy and unrelenting. There were no vacations and no personal leave days. Children were being killed. Beatings were being administered. And there was no labour union to represent the workers.

All of this posed a very significant and sharp question for the people of Israel. They were supposed to be in a special covenant relationship with the God who had called Abraham out of idolatry to be the father of their nation. This nation was to be the vehicle for bringing the Messiah into this world. Why was God allowing them to suffer in such a horrible way?

The question is as old as the human race itself. It never goes away. Even when it is not standing before us to scream at us, it is always lurking in the background. We cannot live very long without it coming back to centre stage.

Why does God allow terrorists to attack? Why does he allow the systematic slaughter of millions of babies? Why are so many without the basic necessities of life?

In addition to all these general questions, are those that pertain to us as individuals. Why did God allow my loved one to die? Why does God allow me to be seriously ill? Why does God allow my children to rebel against me?

These questions, and a thousand more, are so constant and pressing that we often find ourselves depressed about life, disappointed with God and disinclined to serve him.

How are we to respond to the question? Why, indeed, does God allow his people to suffer?

Various answers have been proposed. Many have suggested that God is as troubled by the suffering we are, that he would like to stop it but simply can't. How such a weak and ineffective God is supposed to be powerful enough to make things work out in the end is left unclear by those who take this position.

Others suggest that while God is powerful enough, he is uncaring and unkind. Those who hold this position would have us believe that God takes pleasure from human suffering.

No matter which option we choose – God is not powerful or God is not good – we are left with a God who is not the God of the Bible, which is the same as saying that we are left with no God at all.

How, then, can we retain the teaching of the Bible that God is both powerful and good and explain why he allows his people to suffer?

We can be sure that we will never have in this life a completely satisfactory answer to the problem of evil. We can, however, identify certain truths that help us stay afloat in this sea of evil.

God's purposes

While God has the power to stop suffering, he permits it for purposes that are larger than we can comprehend.

We tend to look at our lives through a single lens, that is, our comfort. How easy it is to regard this as our highest good! When God brings comforting things in to our lives, we conclude that he is doing a good job. When unpleasant circumstances arise, we might conclude that he is failing.

If the premise were correct, the conclusion would be correct. In other words, if God's primary concern is to make our lives comfortable and pleasant, we would be right to be disappointed with him when difficult circumstances arise.

But the Bible goes out of its way to emphasize that his purpose for us is quite different. While God does not delight in our suffering, his purpose is not just to make life in this world easy for us. It is rather to further his plan of redemption. That plan involves saving us from sin and increasingly conforming us to the image of Christ (Rom. 8:29). This purpose requires

God to govern things in an entirely different way than he would if his purpose were to make life comfortable.

It is much easier for us to understand this if we think of our role as parents. If we regard our responsibility as making life as easy and pleasant for our children as possible, we will take a quite different approach to parenting than we will if we understand our role to be that of turning our children into mature adults.

We can rest assured that the Israelites could not see their bondage in Egypt in terms of the larger picture, which was to grow them into a great nation while they were there and to bring them out in mighty, redeeming power. The fact they could not see it did not mean it was not there.

God's discipline

God often permits his people to suffer so they will increasingly turn from the things of the world to him.

It must not escape our notice that the people of Israel 'groaned because of the bondage, and they cried out; and their cry came up to God because of their bondage' (2:23).

Would the Israelites have cried out to God if they had been comfortable in Egypt? We know human nature well enough to answer that. We are so absorbed with ourselves that we do not seek after God until we are desperate for him.

If this is true, namely, that we do not cry out to God until we are desperate, one wonders what kind of calamity it will take to make Christians cry out to God.

God's sympathy

God knows the sorrows of his people and sympathizes with them. The circumstances of the Israelites were such that they may have thought God had no concern for them or had entirely forgotten them.

God is greater than that. He had bound himself to Israel by means of a covenant (2:24), and God does not break his covenants. It was impossible for him to forget about them. In those times in which his people thought he had abandoned them, he was actually there to observe their sufferings, to sympathize with them, and, yes, even to strengthen and sustain them.

God is just as much in covenant with his people today as he was with Israel so long ago. We may be confident, therefore, that he has not forgotten us any more than he did them. The devil is ever anxious to persuade the people of God to draw false conclusions about God. He will point us to our difficulties and assure us that they prove God does not care. We must point him to Calvary's cross as infallible proof that he does care. The wise Christian knows that through the cross God forever answered whether he loves his people, and he, the wise Christian, will never allow his circumstances to call that into question.

God's promise

God will eventually bring the suffering of his people to an end. The Israelites suffered long and hard in Egypt, but there was an end to it. God appeared to Moses in a burning bush and said of his people: 'So I have come down to deliver them out of the hand of the Egyptians, and to bring them up from that land to a good and large land, to a land flowing with milk and honey' (3:8).

Nothing so relieves suffering as knowing that it will eventually give way to a glorious future. And what a future the child of God has – eternal life with God on a new earth with no possibility of pain, suffering or death (Rev. 21)! It is no wonder, then, that Paul wrote: 'For I consider that the sufferings of this present time are not worthy to be compared with the glory which shall be revealed in us' (Rom. 8:18).

The prophecy of Zechariah speaks of a day in which it is 'neither day nor night'. That is the day in which we live. It is a time in which there is a lot of day, that is, a time in which there are many good things to appreciate and enjoy. But it is also a time in which there is a lot of night, that is, a time in which there is much suffering and heartache.

The prophet Zechariah goes on to say: 'But at evening time it shall happen that it will be light' (Zech. 14:7).

How very thankful we should be for that! This mixed time of joy and sorrow will finally come to an end, and the children of God shall only know joy. At evening, it will be light!

The key for us in our suffering is to keep loving and trusting the God who has larger purposes than we understand and who sympathizes with our suffering and to keep looking toward evening.

3 | Behind the scenes

Exodus 2:1-10

The difficulty of bondage in Egypt was for a time softened by the comforts of home. The Israelites were permitted to marry and to have children.

But then came the decree from Pharaoh for his people to kill all the male Israelite babies. What a dark shadow this cast over the Israelites!

This passage turns its spotlight on one Israelite couple. A man of the tribe of Levi married a woman from his tribe. Two children were born to them, and, after Pharaoh's decree, a third child was conceived. Can you imagine the difficulty of those months? Would their baby be a boy or girl? If the baby were a boy, would they be able to protect him or would he become another sad statistic in Pharaoh's systematic slaughter?

It should be a happy day when a couple welcomes a child, but the happiness of this couple was tempered with a feeling of uncertainty. They may have very well fervently hoped for a daughter. And when the midwife announced that it was a boy, their hearts must have trembled. What would they do now? How could they possibly keep this child safe?

This passage presents us with the bare facts. But there is more here than meets the eye. There is no mention of faith, but it is here. There is no mention of God, but he also is here.

The presence of faith

We know that faith was present in this situation because the author of Hebrews says so: 'By faith Moses, when he was born, was hidden three months by his parents, because they saw he was a beautiful child; and they were not afraid of the king's command' (Heb. 11:23).

What is faith? Many Christians seem to equate it with optimism or positive thinking. They believe that it is just a matter of telling ourselves that something is going to be true.

But faith is totally different. It is believing what God has said. There can be no faith where there is no word from God (Rom. 10:17).

When we are told that Moses' parents had faith, then, we are being told that they had received a word from God and that they believed that word.

What word did Moses' parents have? They knew that God had promised to deliver their people from slavery and to bring them back to the land of Canaan (Gen. 17:8; 26:3; 35:12; 46:4; 48:21).

They undoubtedly knew what their forefather Joseph had said on his deathbed: 'I am dying, but God will surely visit you, and bring you out of this land to the land of which He swore to Abraham, to Isaac, and to Jacob …and you shall carry up my bones from here' (Gen. 50:24-25).

In addition to these things, the parents of Moses had a clear indication that the time for their deliverance was drawing nigh (Gen. 15:13-16).

Moses' parents had all of this in common with the other Israelites, but they had something else too. When Moses was born, God evidently gave them a special revelation that this child would become a man who would be used in a special way to bring about the deliverance of the people of Israel.

Our passage tells us that 'he was a beautiful child' (v.2). This phrase is not just telling us that Moses' parents looked upon him with the same feeling that all parents have for their babies. It is telling us that God revealed to them that he had a special plan for Moses. Stephen, in his sermon in Acts 7, says: 'At this time Moses was born, and was well pleasing to God' (Acts 7:20).

Having then both the general revelation of God that their people were to soon be delivered from Egypt, and having the special revelation that their son was to be used of God in this way, the parents of Moses did not give way to despair. They hid Moses for a period of three months, and, when he could no longer be hidden, they made a little ark for him and put him among the bulrushes of the Nile. The river of death (1:22) was to be a river of life for him.

The rest, as they say, is history. Moses was discovered by Pharaoh's daughter who had compassion on him and took him as her own.

All of this must have come to Moses' parents as a terrible that God was indeed going to use their son.

The presence of God

Just as there is no mention of the faith of Moses' parents in our verses, so there is no mention of God. The circumstances of the Israelites were so very distressing and trying that we might be inclined to conclude that God is not mentioned because he had utterly forsaken them. Many of the Israelites themselves probably felt that was the case.

Our own circumstances can become so very harsh and unpleasant that we may very well spend a good bit of our time wondering where God is. But God never abandons his people, and the fact that he is not mentioned does not mean that he is not present and at work.

We have to look no further than the book of Esther to see this. God is mentioned nowhere in the entire book. But there can be no doubt that God was present and at work. He was the one who placed Esther in the position of Queen of Persia. He was the one who used Esther to thwart the scheme of the evil Haman to destroy her people, the Jews. Matthew Henry was certainly correct to say of the book of Esther: 'But though the name of God be not in it, the finger of God is, directing many minute events for the bringing about of his people's deliverance.'[1]

But where is God in these opening verses of Exodus 2? We can find him in several places. First, it was God who gave Moses' parents the revelation that their son would not be killed but would be used to bring about Israel's deliverance.

Secondly, we have to assign the faith of Moses' parents to God. Faith is not something that we can produce within ourselves. It is the gift of God (Eph. 2:8). If Moses' parents believed, it was because God enabled them to believe.

In the next place, we have to attribute each detail of Moses' survival to God. How did Moses' parents come to the idea of putting their baby in an ark on the river? Most parents would have thought the safest place for their babies would have been as far from the river as possible. We have to say that Moses' parents used the river only because God put it in their minds.

And how are we to explain Moses receiving the compassion of Pharaoh's daughter? She knew he was a Hebrew baby (v.6), and she was fully aware of her father's decree. But she was moved with compassion by the baby's cry (v.6) and decided to take him as her own (v.10). And isn't it remarkable that the baby cried at exactly the moment that Pharaoh's daughter opened the little ark? (v.6).

Finally, we have to attribute to God the arrangements that were made by Pharaoh's daughter for the care of the child. Moses' sister, stationed by her parents to watch the ark, was quick to suggest a nurse when Pharaoh's daughter found the baby. Wouldn't you know it! She suggested the baby's mother (vv.7-8).

God has a wonderful sense of humour. He not only saw to it that Moses was cared for by his own mother but that she was paid a salary for doing so! (v.9).

We might be inclined to dismiss all these details as happy coincidences or, as we might say, strokes of good luck. But in God's world, luck has no strokes. What we call luck is nothing less than his sovereign hand guiding and governing the universe that he has created.

What does all this have to do with us? The presence of faith in Moses' parents shows us that real and genuine faith can exist and, yes, even flourish in the most evil of times.

And the presence of God in these events shows us that our faith is not misplaced or mistaken. Even when it appears that God is nowhere near, he is near. And we can trust him to be at work even in evil times to further his plans and to fulfil his promises.

We ourselves live in dark and turbulent times. The devil and the world suggest that we who profess faith might as well give up on God. But it is always too early to give up on God, and what often looks now to be a lost cause will finally prove to be anything but. We must, therefore, keep on trusting and serving God, knowing as we do, that even though we now look very foolish, we shall at last be vindicated.

4 | Moses turns his back on Egypt

Exodus 2:11-15

These verses move us significantly forward in the life of Moses. They take us from the baby in the basket to the young man.

The account is straightforward and matter-of-fact. Moses sees an Egyptian beating an Israelite. He intervenes and kills the Egyptian and buries him in the sand. The next day, as he tries to reconcile two fighting Israelites, one of them confronts him with his killing of the Egyptian. Moses correctly concludes that word of what he had done was getting around. It soon reaches Pharaoh, and Moses is forced to flee to Midian.

Moses, the author of Exodus, presents us with these bare historical facts. We have to go to the book of Hebrews to learn that there was more going on here than him killing an Egyptian and fleeing for his own life.

There we read these words: 'By faith Moses, when he became of age, refused to be called the son of Pharaoh's daughter, choosing rather to suffer affliction with the people of God than to enjoy the passing pleasures of sin, esteeming the reproach of Christ greater riches than the treasures in Egypt; for he looked to the reward. By faith he forsook Egypt, not fearing the wrath of the king; for he endured as seeing Him who is invisible' (Heb. 11:24-27).

While the author of Hebrews does not endorse Moses' killing of the Egyptian, he makes it clear that Moses was making some life-changing choices on the basis of vital spiritual principles. We can get to the heart of these by considering what Moses turned from, what he turned toward, and why he turned as he did.

What Moses turned from

In his wonderful sermon on Hebrews 11:24-27, J.C. Ryle writes of Moses: ' … he made three of the greatest sacrifices that man's heart can possibly make.'[1]

Ryle proceeds to identify these choices as follows: giving up rank and greatness, giving up pleasure and giving up riches.[2] We might say Moses chose to give up privilege, pleasure and possessions.

It was a privilege and honour to be known as 'the son of Pharaoh's daughter' (Heb. 11:24). We can rest assured that this title opened the door to every pleasure Moses or any man could have desired. And it also carried with it the guarantee of incredible wealth. But Moses turned his back on it all.

What Moses turned towards

Moses' choice to turn from his life of privilege, pleasure and riches in Egypt would not be difficult to understand if he had turned toward the same kind of life somewhere else. But, incredibly, Moses turned from these things to embrace a totally different kind of life. We can summarize what the author of Hebrews says about this life by saying it was a life of

+ hardship – 'choosing rather to suffer affliction'
+ association with despised people – 'with the people of God'
+ reproach, scorn and ridicule – 'esteeming the reproach of Christ greater riches'.

Because his choice seems to be so very strange and odd, we must consider...

Why Moses turned as he did

There was no doubt at all in the mind of the author of Hebrews. He says it was all because of Moses' faith (Heb. 11:24, 27).

We can picture it in this way: Moses chose as he did because faith sat on his shoulder and whispered instructions into his ear.

What did faith say to Moses? There is no difficulty here. Faith told Moses –

• that those despised people, the Israelites, were in a special covenant relationship with God and that God had huge plans for them.

• that whatever Egypt could offer him was just for a season, that all the pleasures of sin are 'passing pleasures' (Heb. 11:25).

• that the afflictions and sufferings he, Moses, would have to endure could not begin to compare with the glory which would be his.

• that the reproach and scorn he would have to endure was 'the reproach of Christ' (Heb. 11:26), that whatever he, Moses, did for the people of God, he did for the Lord Jesus Christ himself and whatever he suffered in the doing, he suffered for Christ.

By the way, isn't it interesting that the author of Hebrews attributes faith in Christ to Moses? We shouldn't be surprised by this. The people of the Old Testament knew about the Lord Jesus Christ. They were given promises that he would come to this earth and that his coming would be for the purpose of making an atonement for sinners. And the people of the Old Testament period were saved by looking forward in faith to that coming.

Faith, then, whispered all these things – and more! – in the ear of Moses. And Moses heard what faith had to say, believed it and acted upon it. When he tallied it all up, he realized that he was giving up little in Egypt and gaining much.

Many down through the centuries have made choices similar to that which Moses made. Missionary Jim Elliot comes to mind. He determined that he would take the gospel of Christ to the Auca Indians in Ecuador.

This venture cost him his life. The very Indians he desired to see saved took his life.

Many would call Jim Elliot a fool. Let's allow him to answer that indictment: 'He is no fool who gives what he cannot keep to gain what he cannot lose.'[3]

Jim Elliot was willing to lay down life in this world, which he could not keep, if by doing so, he could be of service to Christ and, in the words of the book about his life, be received *Through Gates of Splendor*.

We must not forget that Moses made his choice when he was young. Now here is the burden of my heart: very few young people who profess Christ seem to be making the choices that Moses made. In fact, they appear to be making the opposite choices. They profess to know Christ and to love Christ, but they choose evil company and evil habits. If pressed to the wall, they would find it very hard to identify a single time in which they chose for Christ rather than for pleasure or possessions.

Why are there so few young people who are making heroic choices for Christ? Many simply do not know Christ. They went forward in a church service and made their profession at that age at which most children of church members do the same. They went forward as sort of a cultural thing, as something that they were expected to do at that time. But there was never any real repentance and never any real attachment of their hearts to Christ.

To this we can add that many of our young people are the way they are because of the way we adults are. They see us putting other things ahead of Christ and they conclude that the things of this world must be very important and Christ and his work must be very unimportant. It is not surprising that our young people put other things above Christ when they frequently see adults doing the same.

The choice of Moses to turn away from the things of the world and to turn toward the things of God calls all of us to thoroughly examine ourselves.

Are we listening to the voice of faith? It is saying the same things now as it did to Moses! Do we hear it speaking about the fleeting nature of the things of this world? Do we hear it speaking about the incredible glory that awaits the children of God?

How are we responding to the voice of faith? Are we making choices that reflect what we profess, or are we making choices that undercut our profession?

All who are inclined to tune out the voice of faith to embrace this passing world would do well to ponder these words from the Lord Jesus Christ: 'Do not lay up for yourselves treasures on earth, where moth and rust destroy and where thieves break in and steal, but lay up for yourselves treasures in heaven, where neither moth nor rust destroys and where thieves do not break in and steal. For where you treasure is, there your heart will be also' (Matt. 6:19-21).

5 | The university of the burning bush

Exodus 3:1-8

Moses was about as far from the centre of things as a man could get. He was not in Egypt but in Midian. There he was not involved in some sort of strategic work, but rather with the tending of the sheep of his father-in-law.

While still in Egypt, Moses had been very zealous for the people of Israel, but he had now been in Midian for forty years (Acts 7:30). He seemed to be on the fast track to nowhere. He may very well have long since concluded that God had no plans for him, that he would live out his days in obscurity. He couldn't have been more wrong.

One day his shepherding took him to Mt. Horeb, which is identified as 'the mountain of God' (v.2). Mt. Horeb was another name for Mt. Sinai, which would play such a prominent part in the life of Moses and the people of Israel.

Suddenly Moses saw something of an eye-popping nature. A bush was burning without being consumed.

Moses was destined to see many remarkable things, but he would never see anything more astonishing than this.

The burning bush was not given to Moses just so he could be astonished. It was not given for him to have a sensational experience. It was rather given so that he could learn some vital lessons that would sustain him throughout his remaining years. Moses had been educated with the best Egypt had to offer, but he was about to attend a university which was unlike any other, that is, the university of the burning bush. Egypt had no school that could compare with this.

First, the burning bush taught Moses about...

The nature of God

Moses knew about God. He knew that God had called his ancestor Abraham out of idolatry and had made him the father of a new nation, Israel. He knew that God had called Abraham and that nation into a special covenant relationship with himself. He knew that the centrepiece of that relationship was the promise of the coming Messiah. Moses, as we have noted previously, looked forward in faith to the Messiah.

But while Moses had all this information about God, there was still much for him to know. No one ever knows all there is to know about the true God!

What did this bush reveal about God? It certainly revealed something of his sovereign power. His power was such that he could override the laws of nature by making a bush burn without it perishing.

The bush also revealed something of the self-sufficiency of God. God himself was like that bush. He is never used up with all that he does. His strength is never depleted. His wisdom is never diminished. His grace is never lessened. With all that God has done in the past, he is still fully God. He is sufficient for us as much as he was for Moses and the people of Israel.

The bush also revealed the holy nature of God. As Moses began to approach, 'the Angel of the Lord appeared to him in a flame of fire from the midst of a bush' (v.2).

We have here a miracle within a miracle. The first is the bush burning without being consumed. The second is the Angel of the Lord appearing in the burning bush.

When we see this term 'the Angel of the Lord', we are probably to understand that the Lord Jesus Christ himself was making what is called 'a pre-incarnate appearance.' In other words, the second person of the Trinity appears long before he would actually step into human history in the form of Jesus of Nazareth.

We can well imagine Moses' desire to draw closer to get a better view of this sight (v.3). But as he drew near, the Angel of the Lord said: 'Do not draw near this place. Take your sandals off your feet, for the place where you stand is holy ground' (v.5).

God is of such a holy nature that the very ground he touches is made holy, and the slightest particle of dirt from Moses' sandals would contaminate that ground.

The God who appeared here is still holy. He is completely without moral contamination. He is perfect in every way without any flaw or sin.

Moses would have been well blessed that day if he had learned nothing more than these things. But the bush had more to teach him. It also showed him something about...

The situation of his people

As he stood there staring at the burning bush, Moses could not help but think of his people. They were even at that moment in a furnace of fire in Egypt, a furnace of affliction. But they would not be consumed by it!

The God who was appearing there in the bush also spoke to Moses: 'I have surely seen the oppression of My people who are in Egypt, and have heard their cry because of their taskmasters, for I know their sorrows' (v.7).

The furnace of affliction could not destroy the people of Israel because God had bound himself to them by covenant. That is the reason he said to Moses: 'I am the God your father — the God of Abraham, the God of Isaac, and the God of Jacob' (v.6).

The university today

What does all this have to do with us? We might say that burning bush is still a university in which we need to enrol. It speaks to us, even as it did to Moses, about the greatness of our God and the need to reverence him.

No truth is more urgently needed by the church. This is the day of easy and breezy familiarity with God. There seems to be little consciousness of how great God is and how unworthy we are.

The burning bush also speaks to us about God sustaining his people. The church in every age experiences the fires of suffering. Sometimes it seems as if she will cease to exist. We may rest assured that she will not be destroyed no matter how much she suffers because the Lord himself is in the midst of her.

We should also apply this on the personal level. The fires of temptation, affliction and difficulty often burn in the lives of individual Christians, but God has promised that these things cannot destroy us. God will bring each one of his people home to heaven. Not one will be missing.

While God's people can indeed be likened to bushes that burn without being consumed, I must go on to say that there are bushes that will most certainly be consumed (John 15:6). The fires of affliction cannot destroy the Christian because God is with him and within him, but those who have never come to saving faith in Jesus Christ do not have this protection. The most important business in life for the unbeliever, then, is to flee to Christ for salvation while there is still time to do so.

While we are on this matter of salvation, I have to say that I see yet another dimension to the burning bush, namely, an anticipation or picture of the Lord Jesus Christ and his redeeming work. I am not necessarily saying that Moses saw this (although I would not be surprised if he did). But looking back at the burning bush from our vantage point, we can see these parallels:

+ As God stooped to reveal himself in that lowly desert shrub, so the Lord Jesus Christ stooped to take unto himself our humanity.

Henry Law says of Christ: 'He is God, and yet He stoops to be made man. He is man, and yet He continues to be God for ever. Withdraw the Godhead, and His blood cannot atone. Withdraw the manhood, and no blood remains. The union gives a Saviour able, and a Saviour meet. Look to the Bush. It shows this very union. The wood denotes the poor and feeble produce of earth ... . But it holds God as its inmate.'[1]

Is that not a picture of the incarnation of Christ? He took our feeble humanity and allowed it to hold him as its inmate.

+ As fire enveloped the bush, so Christ was enveloped by sufferings in his life and in his death.
+ As the fire could not destroy the bush, so Christ was not de-

stroyed by his sufferings but arose from the grave in triumph over them all.

This is the Christ that now freely offers himself to all. I appeal to those who have not received him to do so. Do not be one of those bushes that will be burned in judgement. The Lord Jesus went to the cross for the express purpose of receiving God's judgement in the place of sinners. Take him as Saviour, and you will never have to fear experiencing God's judgement yourself.

6 | Please excuse me!

Exodus 3:9-4:17

After appearing to Moses in the burning bush, the Lord promised to deliver his people from their bondage in Egypt (3:7-8).

This promise undoubtedly caused Moses to rejoice. Then the other foot fell: 'Come now, therefore, and I will send you to Pharaoh that you may bring My people, the children of Israel, out of Egypt' (3:10).

This was not what Moses wanted to hear. Yes, he wanted Israel to be delivered, but he didn't want to be the one through whom it was accomplished. The memory of his failed attempt to be a deliverer years before probably came flooding into his mind (Exod. 2:11-15; Acts 7:23-28).

Excuse #1

So Moses began to make excuses. His first excuse was: 'Who am I that I should go to Pharaoh, and that I should bring the children of Israel out of Egypt?' (3:11).

This was the excuse of unworthiness. And the Lord's answer to it was: 'I will certainly be with you' (3:12).

Moses had to learn that he was being sent, not because he himself was adequate for the task, but rather because the God who was sending him was adequate for him.

Moses' first excuse has not died. When called to serve the Lord, many immediately say: 'I am not worthy!'

What such people fail to realize is that no one who serves the Lord is worthy of doing so. And they also fail to understand that the Lord delights in using unworthy people.

Someone has pointed out that Moses' life falls into three major stages. The first forty years, he spent thinking he was somebody. The second he spent learning that he was nobody. And the third forty he spent finding out what God can do with a nobody.

Excuse #2

The Lord's response to Moses' first excuse should have been sufficient. If the Lord is for us, who can be against us? But Moses was not about to give up so easily. The loss of excuse #1 only prompted him to offer excuse #2 - 'Indeed, when I come to the children of Israel and say to them "The God of your fathers has sent me to you," and they say to me, "What is His name?" what shall I say to them?' (3:13).

This is the excuse of ignorance. Moses was saying: 'I don't know what to say.'

But God would not let Moses off the hook. He responded: 'I AM WHO I AM. ... Thus you shall say to the children of Israel, "I AM has sent me to you"' (3:14).

God removed this excuse as quickly as the first. Moses was to tell the people that 'I AM WHO I AM' had sent him.

This, God's personal name which he had not before revealed, declared at one and the same time his self-existence, his immutability and his eternity.

God is self-existent. He does not need anything or draw from anything for his existence. He is autonomous and independent.

God is immutable. He is what he has always been. He is not in the process of becoming something else.

God is eternal. He will always be what he has been and what he is.

What consolation there is in this name! When the people of Israel asked about the one who sent Moses, they would be told that it was no one less than the almighty, eternal God. Pharaoh was no match for such a God!

We should not leave this point without recalling that the Lord Jesus Christ appropriated the name 'I AM' for himself, affirming in doing so that he was God in human flesh. Seven times in John's gospel, he attached to the name 'I AM' some glorious part of his person and work: the bread of life, the light of the world, the door, the good shepherd, the resurrection and the life, the vine, and the way, the truth and the life.

Excuse #3

We should think that the glory of what Moses had seen and heard up to this point would have caused him to stop objecting and fall in worship before the Lord. But he is not through. Here is his next excuse: 'But suppose they will not believe me or listen to my voice; suppose they say, "The Lord has not appeared to you"' (4:1). This is the excuse of doubt.

God answered this objection by giving Moses two signs on the spot and promising him that he would be able to perform a third sign. The first two signs are as follows:

> ✦ turning his rod into a serpent and then into a rod again (4:2-4). The centrepiece of Pharaoh's head-dress was a raised cobra. With this particular sign, the Lord would assure Israel that he was greater than Pharaoh and the snake-gods he worshipped.

> ✦ causing his hand to be leprous and then whole again (4:5-8). With this sign the Lord would affirm that he had the power to rescue Israel from the leprosy of bondage and make her a nation again.

The sign that God promised to give Moses was pouring out water from the Nile which would become blood on the ground (4:9). The Egyptians considered the Nile to be their life-giver. This sign would prove that the Lord had sovereignty over Egypt.

The fact that God gave these miracles at this point tells us something about the nature of miracles. They were not given to make life more comfortable and easy or to satisfy a craving for the sensational but rather to attest to the authority God was investing in Moses.

This was, by the way, the same reason for the miracles of Jesus. While they did relieve suffering, they were primarily for the purpose of proving that he was indeed the Messiah.

By giving Moses these signs the Lord was assuring him that he, the Lord, was more than sufficient for the situation into which he was sending Moses.

The church today is called to preach the gospel of Christ in cultures that are increasingly disinclined to believe. The church often responds to this by toning down her message and offering entertaining programs that have little to do with Christianity. The need of this hour is for the people of God to again understand that God is sufficient for our situation and to seek his face.

Excuse #4

Here is the final excuse Moses offered: 'O my Lord, I am not eloquent, neither before nor since You have spoken to Your servant; but I am slow of speech and slow of tongue' (4:10).

This is the excuse of inability. It is an excuse with which every preacher of the gospel is familiar.

God answered this objection by saying: 'Who has made man's mouth? … Now therefore, go, and I will be with your mouth and teach you what you shall say' (4:11a, 12).

The point is again the sufficiency of God. What God calls us to do he enables us to do.

God's promise to help Moses should have been sufficient for him, but Moses was weak in faith and insisted that the Lord send someone else (4:13). It should encourage us to know that even the heroes of the faith often struggled.

The Lord graciously consented to send Moses' brother Aaron, a good speaker, to help Moses (4:14-16).

Aaron did indeed go with Moses, but, interestingly enough, we seldom read of Aaron speaking, a fact which indicates that Moses soon learned that God was indeed sufficient for him.

God has always used common, ordinary, unskilled people to do his work. John Bunyan, an ordinary mender of pots and pans, was used by the Lord to write The Pilgrim's Progress and other powerful works.

This caused A.W. Pink to observe: 'God has used the simple language of unlettered Bunyan far more than he has the polished writings of thousands of University graduates!'[1]

We have seen, then, how Moses raised excuses and the Lord dismantled each one. What about us? The Lord has work for us to do just as he had for Moses. Are we doing that work, or are we taking refuge in excuses? Our excuses may seem to be legitimate now, but when we finally come into the presence of the Lord and see his glory we shall also see how pathetic our excuses really were. Our profound regret when we are confronted with the glory of our God will be that we only had one life on this earth with which to serve him and we did not use it to its fullest. The excuses that comfort us now will only shame us then.

7 | Moses runs into trouble

Exodus 5:1-6:8

This passage does not paint a pretty picture. Here we have Moses doing as God commanded only to get nowhere.

Shouldn't faithfulness to God bring blessing? We would like to think so. For Moses it brought difficulty. We might say he went from the burning bush to burning trials.

Moses does not stand alone. Many others in Scripture (e.g. Noah, Daniel, Elijah) and in history have found obedience to God to yield hardship.

William Kirk Kilpatrick writes: 'God did not create a simple world, and He has not given us a simple religion ... . Still, you will come across some Christians who want to boil it down to a few formulas as though the way of faith were a simple thing like a recipe for apple turnover. You find ministers of the Word who have reduced the gospel message to the social gospel, or to the gospel of success, or to the gospel of positive thinking, or who have reduced Christ to the level of a good business partner.'[1]

Careful study of this passage will help rescue us from the tendency to make the Christian life easy and from the temptation to think that our faithfulness will bring us no hardships.

As we look at this passage, we note Moses' two imposing problems and his sufficient resource.

Moses' two problems

We can identify the first of these as...

The contempt of an unbelieving world

Moses and Aaron presented their demand to Pharaoh with these words: 'Thus says the Lord God of Israel: "Let My people go, that they may hold a feast to Me in the wilderness"' (5:1).

Pharaoh responded: 'Who is the Lord, that I should obey His voice to let Israel go? I do not know the Lord, nor will I let Israel go' (5:2).

The Pharaoh before whom Moses stood considered himself something of an expert on gods. He considered himself to be one. He was called 'The Son of the Sun.' In addition to Pharaoh, Egypt had approximately eighty other gods.

When Moses and Aaron began speaking about the God of Israel, Pharaoh essentially said: 'I have the list of gods right here, and yours is not on the list.'

In addition to that, there did not seem to be much about the God of Moses to commend him. Pharaoh knew visible gods that were successful. Ra, the sun god, was a blazing success each day as he made his way across the sky. And Hopi, the Nile goddess, was a success each year when the Nile overflowed its banks.

But Moses and Aaron were asking him to obey an invisible God whose people had been in bondage for 430 years. An invisible God of slaves! The very idea was absurd as far as Pharaoh was concerned.

The God of Israel earned Pharaoh's contempt even more by the demand that he was making. It ran counter to Pharaoh and his demands. Pharaoh wanted more bricks in less time, and this God was wanting worship!

God's agenda colliding with the agenda of this world! It has always been and will continue to be as long as the world stands. Every Christian knows about this. Giving priority to God's agenda inevitably brings hostility from the Pharaohs of this world who seek to silence the voice of the eternal God by focusing on the temporal bricks of this life.

If Moses was shocked by Pharaoh's response, he was in for an even larger shock. His demand to Pharaoh led to a second problem, namely...

The unhappiness of his own people

Pharaoh responded to Moses and Aaron's request by laying a heavier workload on the people of Israel. In addition to having to make the same number of bricks each day, they would also have to gather their own straw (5:10-19).

This caused the officers or foremen of the people of Israel to speak these harsh words to Moses and Aaron: 'Let the Lord look on you and judge because you have made us abhorrent in the sight of Pharaoh and in the sight of his servants, to put a sword in their hand to kill us' (5:21).

These foremen had become so accustomed to the reality of Pharaoh that there was no room in their minds and hearts for the possibility of God doing something extraordinary. They were so busy with the temporal that they could not see the eternal. They speak to us about the terribly possibility of getting so occupied with the bricks of life that we cannot feel the breeze of the Spirit.

Moses' sufficient resource

Driven to the brink of despair, Moses cried out: 'Lord, why have You brought trouble on this people? Why is it You have sent me? For since I came to Pharaoh to speak in Your name, he has done evil to this people; neither have You delivered Your people at all' (5:22b-23).

God could have sternly rebuked Moses for his lack of faith, but instead He encouraged his weak servant by asserting the following:

+ Pharaoh's first reaction was not to be taken as his final reaction. Pharaoh was completely in God's hand and would in God's time not only release the people but would actually 'drive' them away (6:1).

+ God had not changed since he revealed himself to Moses at the burning bush. He was still the 'I AM,' that is, he was totally sufficient for what had to be done (6:2).

+ God would not be unfaithful to his promises. He had formed a covenant with Abraham, Isaac, and Jacob, a covenant which included giving their descendants the land of Canaan. Nothing could cause God to forget that covenant (6:4-5).

+ God had a compassion for his people that would not allow them to continue in agony in Egypt (6:5).

Moses was to relate to the people, then, not what he thought about their situation or how he assessed their future, but rather what God had to say about their situation and their future.

God's message to the people was dominated by two phrases: 'I will' (appearing eight times) and 'I am' (appearing three times). It is interesting to note that the 'I will' statements are bracketed by two of the 'I am' statements (6:6,8). The promises of God are certain because they are based on the greatness of his person. Because of that Moses could rest assured of the accomplishment of God's purpose.

When the 'I AM' says 'I will', there can be no room for doubt or discouragement.

The 'I will' statements are broad in scope. They began with the Israelites in miserable bondage and take them from that bondage into an unspeakably wonderful future. That future is conveyed in these promises:

+ God would take them to himself for a special people and would be their God (6:7)

+ They would know that he was their mighty God (6:8).

+ He would bring them into the land he had promised them and would give it to them as their heritage (6:8).

These 'I will' statements, then, embody two elements: what they were to be saved from and what they were to be saved to. We can, of course, relate these two elements to our own salvation. We are saved from God's wrath and eternal condemnation, but we are also saved to certain things: fellowship with God and with God's people, adoption into God's family, the presence of the Holy Spirit and eternal glory in heaven.

We know how the story of Moses and Pharaoh ends. Equipped with the assurance provided by these two phrases, Moses stayed faithful, and the people of Israel were released from their bondage in Egypt.

But it was not because Moses suddenly became sufficient for the task. And it was not because the people of Israel suddenly became co-operative and supportive. And it was not because Pharaoh abruptly became soft-hearted and agreeable. It was rather because the God, who had bound himself to Israel, showed himself strong on her behalf.

8 | Serpents and plagues

Exodus 7:1-10:29

These are some of the most remarkable chapters in the Bible. They begin with Aaron's rod becoming a serpent and then proceed to describe the first nine plagues that God unleashed on Pharaoh and the people of Egypt.

These chapters report, therefore, an explosion of miracles. We cannot encounter the miracles of the Bible without also encountering a very controversial question: should the people of God be seeing such miracles today?

Many do not hesitate to say that we should. They are also quick to assure us that it is entirely our own fault if we are not, that is, it is due to us not having sufficient faith.

Those who hold this position fail to understand that the miracles of the Bible fall into four periods: (1) the time of Moses (2) the era of Elijah and Elisha (3) the time of captivity (4) the time of Christ and the early church. These were periods of crisis in which God was moving in a special way to further his cause. Put them all together and they represent a very small portion of all the years covered by the Bible.

Others, of course, take the opposite view and say that the miracles described in the Bible did not take place at all. This view essentially denies that God can step into the world he made and override the laws he put into place. In the final analysis, their problem is not with the miracles but with the God of the miracles.

These are extreme views. The truth is that the miracles of the Bible did take place, but they took place intermittently.

As important as the subject of miracles is, we must not get so caught up with it that we miss the spiritual truths that are set before us in these chapters. These truths are just as important now as they were at that time.

The sovereignty of God

When Moses and Aaron stood for the second time before Pharaoh, they were also standing on the front edge of one of history's most dazzling displays of God's sovereignty and glory.

God first demonstrated this sovereignty when Pharaoh demanded that Moses and Aaron give him a sign. Aaron responded by doing as God had commanded, that is, by throwing his rod to the ground whereupon it immediately turned into a serpent.

Pharaoh responded to this by calling his own magicians in to do the same. But Aaron's serpent swallowed the serpents of Pharaoh's magicians (7:12).

We will not appreciate the significance of this if we do not keep in mind that the serpent was the emblem of Pharaoh and his power. His head-dress featured a raised cobra. The fact that Aaron's serpent devoured the others amounted to nothing less than God declaring his supremacy over Pharaoh.

The ten plagues were God's way of asserting his supremacy over all the gods of Egypt. The first plague consisted of the water of the Nile turning to blood. The Egyptians worshipped the Nile. By turning its water to blood, God was demonstrating his supremacy over the Nile and making their own god repugnant and repulsive to them.

One after another more plagues come – frogs, lice, flies, diseased livestock, boils, hail, locusts, darkness, and with each plague it is crystal clear that the God of Israel is in control and the gods of Egypt are powerless to do anything about it.

The sovereign God who demonstrated his might over the gods of Egypt is the God with whom we are dealing.

The justice of God

The plagues God sent upon Egypt did more than demonstrate his sovereignty. They also served as his just judgements upon the Egyptians for their cruel treatment of the Israelites and for their unfeeling slaughter of male babies (Exod. 1:22). Because God does not immediately send judgement upon us for our sins, we have the tendency to think we are getting by with them. But no one ever finally gets away with sin, and God's judgement will eventually fall.

The plagues which God sent upon Egypt are miniature pictures of what he will send upon unbelievers at the end of time (Rev.16). At that time people will cry for the rocks and mountains to cover them (Rev.6:16), but there will be no escape. Pastors labour diligently now to get people to see the greatness and the justice of God. All too often our efforts seem to be to no avail. On that day, no one will need to be told how awesome God is and how firm his justice is. All will know it very well.

The ability of Satan to counterfeit

The chapters before us also remind us of the reality of Satan and the ability he has to counterfeit the work of God. This is evident when Pharaoh's magicians turned their rods into serpents (Exod. 7:11).

Some think these magicians used sleight of hand to produce serpents. One theory is that by tightly pinching serpents behind their heads, the magicians could make them rigid like sticks. According to this theory, the rods were serpents all along and merely looked like rods while the magicians firmly held them.

This view fails to adequately address the teaching of Scripture about the power of Satan. It must be noted that Christians are not 'dualists.' We do not believe that Satan is equal to God and that the outcome is in doubt. And we cannot say with complete certainty why God allows Satan to exercise such power. That, along with all other mysteries, awaits the clarification that will come in eternity.

Having said all that, we do know that Satan is such a powerful and clever foe that he is indeed able to perform signs and wonders. This is, in fact, how the anti-Christ will be able to deceive so many (2 Thess. 2:9). Satan is not to be taken lightly but is rather to be resisted by the power of God and by being clothed with the armour that God provides (Eph. 6:10-20).

The hardness of the unbelieving heart

A fourth truth we encounter as we look at the miracle of the serpent and the plagues that followed is the incredible hardness of the human heart.

The hardness of Pharaoh's heart is described in three ways. In some places we are simply told that it 'grew hard' (7:13,22; 8:19; 9:7). In other places we are told that Pharaoh 'hardened his heart' (8:15,32; 9:24). And in other places we are told that God hardened the heart of Pharaoh (9:12; 10:20,27).

When we put these things together we arrive at this truth – when people harden their hearts against God, he, God, judges them by hardening their hearts even more.

God did not create evil within Pharaoh, but, as an act of just judgement, God did give Pharaoh over to the spirit of rebellion that was at work within him.

What a solemn reminder this is to all who hear the gospel and harden their hearts against it! Those who reject God long enough invite him to harden their hearts against the truth.

The grace of God

We should be grateful that the accounts of Aaron's serpent and the plagues yield yet another truth, namely, the gracious nature of God towards his people.

The people of Israel had been in such desperate conditions for such a long time that they must have often felt as if God did not exist or that he did not care about them. As the plagues began to unfold, the people of Israel could not help but understand that God was showing himself strong on their behalf.

We encounter many of the same feelings with which the Israelites of old were so familiar. Evil mounts up around us and persecution becomes more prevalent. It is enough to make us cry out 'Where is God?'

We cannot speak with finality about the ways and the timing of God. These things are locked up in the secret counsels of heaven. But we can say with assurance that God never forgets his people and will in his own time and way deliver them from all evil. It is not ours to figure God out. It is ours to trust him and serve him while we wait for that day when dark things will be made plain.

9 | The Passover

Exodus 11:1-12:30

Nine plagues have come and gone, and Pharaoh has refused to humble himself before God and let the people of Israel go.

But God cannot be defeated. It often appears that he has been, but that is always in appearance only. The only ones who attribute failure to God are those who fail to correctly perceive his sovereign power and wisdom.

God is never at a loss about what to do. Pharaoh's stubborn resistance did not befuddle God or send him into a panic. The victory was secure from the very beginning. Pharaoh would not let the people go until God finished pouring plagues out upon Egypt, and God would not finish with those plagues until he had established the Passover.

God announced the last plague to Moses in these words: 'I will bring yet one more plague on Pharaoh and on Egypt. Afterward he will let you go from here. When he lets you go, he will surely drive you out of here altogether' (11:1).

There is absolutely no uncertainty in those words. God does not say that he has tried and tried to find a way and he is down to this last desperate measure which he now hopes will work. No, it was all determined in advance. Pharaoh would not let the people go until God had his Passover.

The Passover is an event of such monumental significance that it is absolutely essential for us to understand it. Let's seek to do so by looking at the following: the devastating announcement, the special provision and a glorious picture.

A devastating announcement (11:4-6)

After the ninth plague came to an end, Pharaoh once again called for Moses (10:24). This meeting ended with Moses speaking these words: 'Thus says the Lord: "About midnight I will go out into the midst of Egypt; and all the firstborn of Egypt shall die, from the firstborn of Pharaoh who sits on his throne, even to the firstborn of the maidservant who is behind the handmill, and all the firstborn of the beasts. Then there shall be a great cry throughout all the land of Egypt, such as was not like it before, nor shall be like it again"' (11:4-6).

This promise of a tenth and final plague raises some perplexing questions. The first is this: how could God do such a thing? The short answer is that this constituted just judgement upon the Egyptians for their cruel treatment of the Israelite people and, specifically, for their merciless slaughter of the Israelite infants (1:13-14,22).

A second question is this: Why did God target the firstborn? He did so because the firstborn represented strength and dignity to the people of that time (Gen. 49:3; Ps. 78:51). The Egyptians were very proud of themselves and their culture, but by this plague God would break their strength and humble them.

We must not read this as though it were a meaningless slice of ancient history. The truth is we are all by nature under a sentence of death. We come into this world with a built-in pride. We feel self-sufficient, thinking we can live without regard to God and his laws.

Meanwhile God says if we continue to live like this and without submitting to him, we will experience eternal wrath and destruction. In other words, God promises to give us in eternity what we have chosen in life. If we live here without making room for God, he will see to it that we live in eternity without him.

While justice and wrath are certainly part of the truth about God, they are by no means the only truths. This passage also affords us the opportunity to note...

God's special provision (12:1-13)

God's death sentence against the firstborn included all those in the land of Egypt. Even the firstborn of the people of Israel would have been slain had it not been for the special provision God made for his people.

What was this provision? We find the answer in these words: '... every man shall take for himself a lamb, ... ' (12:3).

As we read the verses that follow, we note several things about this lamb:

+ It had to be the right size, that is, it had be large enough to feed each member of the family. If a family was too small to eat the lamb, they could share it with a neighbour (12:4).

+ It had to be the right age (12:5). The lamb had to be in the prime of its life. The people were not to use an old, feeble sheep.

+ It had to be without blemish (12:5). The lamb could not be crippled or damaged in any way. In keeping with this particular requirement, the lamb had to be carefully observed for four days (12:3,6).

+ It had to be slain (12:6). Keeping the lamb alive and taking it into the house on the night of the Passover would not be sufficient. By slaying the lamb, the people would be saying that the firstborn deserved to die for their sins, but they were offering the lamb instead. The lamb would receive as their substitute the death the firstborn deserved to die.

+ The blood of the lamb had to be applied to the top and the sides of their doors (12:7).

+ Each Israelite was to stay in his house marked with the blood and eat all the roasted flesh of the lamb along with unleavened bread and bitter herbs (12:8-10). Furthermore, they were to eat it quickly and with readiness to travel (12:11).

The bitter herbs were to serve as a reminder of their years of bitter slavery in Egypt. The bread was to be unleavened because there was not time to allow the yeast to work in the dough.

Having given these instructions to the people of Israel, God gave them this unspeakably glorious promise: ' ... when I see the blood, I will pass over you; and the plague shall not be on you to destroy you when I strike the land of Egypt' (12:13).

God did just as he promised. All the firstborn of Egypt died (12:29-30), but the people of Israel were passed over. The lamb made the difference!

Christians cannot read this ancient account without their hearts leaping within. They know that there is much more here than a description of the provision God made for the Israelites. There is also here –

A glorious picture

Christians rejoice over this account because they see Christ and their own salvation wonderfully pictured.

Christians know, as we have noted, that they were rightfully and justly under God's sentence of eternal death just as was the case with the land of Egypt. But the same God who had pronounced this sentence had also made a way of escape. That way is his Son, Jesus Christ.

We must be clear about this: the Lord Jesus Christ came into this world in the capacity of the Lamb of God (John 1:29). He came to receive the eternal death that his people themselves deserved. He came to receive it so they would not have to receive it. He came to receive it so that God would not visit his eternal judgement upon them but rather would pass over them.

As the lamb of God, the Lord was the right size, that is, he is the sufficient Saviour for all who believe. No one who believes in Christ needs anything or anyone except Christ.

The Lord Jesus was also offered in the prime of his life, in the fullness of his strength. And he was also offered without defect. There was absolutely no sin in Christ. Had there been, he could not have been the sinless dying for the sinful but rather the sinful dying for his own sins (1 Peter 1:19; 1 John 3:5).

And, of course, as the lamb of God, the Lord Jesus was slain. He shed his blood on the cross. The law of God requires that the sinner die, and Jesus died. He could not save us by setting a good example for us to follow or by offering teachings for us to understand. He could only save us by paying the penalty for our sins.

There is still more. The blood of Christ has to be individually applied. If we want God to pass over us and not visit us in judgement, we must appropriate the redeeming work of Christ by faith. It is not enough to know that Jesus died on the cross, we must personally trust in what he did there. The Israelites were not saved from death merely because they had been born Israelites, and we are not saved from eternal wrath because we have been born into a Christian family or because we have been brought up in church.

After we have been saved, we must continue to feed on Christ. We must eat the bitter herbs, remembering the bondage of our sin, and we must eat the unleavened bread, that is, remember that we are called as Christians not to settle down in this world as if we are permanent residents but rather to travel lightly as pilgrims.

The apostle Paul calls Christ 'our Passover' (1 Cor. 5:7), and so he is. We have all we need in Christ to escape the judgement of God. Believer in Christ, rejoice! Unbeliever, if you want God to pass over you on Judgement Day, trust now in Christ.

10 Good things to know about God

Exodus 13:17-22

The execution of the firstborn of Egypt achieved the purpose for which it was designed. This catastrophic event prompted Pharaoh to call for Moses and Aaron in the night. So anxious was he to get rid of the Israelites that he could not wait for daylight. When Moses and Aaron arrived, Pharaoh said: 'Rise and go out from among my people, both you and the children of Israel. And go, serve the Lord as you have said' (12:31).

When we come to the verses of our text, we find that the Israelites have begun their journey out of Egypt. But the value of these verses is not to be found in the few details they give of the beginning of Israel's journey, but rather in what they tell us about God.

We must never read the Bible as mere history. The biblical authors are set on telling us that there is much more to human history than humans. God is always at work, so much so that someone observed that history is in fact 'His-story.' What then do these verses tell us about God?

The first thing is this:

God is not primarily concerned about our comfort and convenience

If God had been concerned with the comfort of the people of Israel and had wanted to make things easy for them, he would have led them 'by the way of the land of the Philistines' (v.17).

The way through Philistia was the shortest way and it appeared to be the most convenient way. But God would not allow his people to use it. He knew that it would mean war before the people were ready to face war, and he knew such a war would cause them to return to Egypt (v.17).

So it was the long way around for the people of Israel.

All of this has immense relevance for us. We often have difficulty understanding the circumstances in which we find ourselves. If those circumstances are particularly difficult, we may even allow ourselves to feel disappointed or angry with God.

Many of us assume something to which we are not entitled, that is, that God wants to make our lives as comfortable and easy as he possibly can. If this is our assumption, we cannot help but conclude that God has failed when our circumstances go sour.

But the problem is not that God has failed. It is rather that we do not understand his purpose for our lives. It is not to make us comfortable but to make us spiritually mature. With this as his purpose it is necessary for him to take an entirely different approach with us than he would if he were only seeking our ease.

A second thing we learn from these verses is that...

God loves order

Verse 18 says: 'And the children of Israel went up in orderly ranks out of the land of Egypt.'

We are not to picture the people of Israel leaving Egypt in helter-skelter fashion or in an 'every man for himself' mode.

This must come as a keen disappointment to many. A popular notion is that God loves chaos, and we are most spiritual when we throw order aside. The impression we are given these days is that God is most pleased with us when nothing has been planned and when we show casual irreverence in his house.

Those who hold such a view would do well to look around them. If God loves chaos and lack of order, why does creation reflect such precision and order?

They would also do well to reflect on some of the most ignored words in the Bible: 'Let all things be done decently and in order' (1 Cor. 14:40).

A third truth that emerges from these verses is most precious indeed, namely,

God keeps his promises

Verse 19 powerfully drives this truth home with these simple words: 'And Moses took the bones of Joseph with him…'

We well remember the story of Joseph. He was the Israelite who rose to prominence in the land of Egypt. He was the reason that the Israelites settled in Egypt (Gen. 39-50).

Although Joseph spent 93 of his 110 years in Egypt, he wanted to be buried in the land of Canaan. It was not mere sentiment that caused him to desire this. It was rather a strong expression of his faith. Joseph knew that his people would not remain in Egypt. He knew that God would eventually deliver them and bring them into the land of Canaan (Gen. 50:24-25). He knew that the Messiah would live and die and rise again in that land.

How did Joseph know these things? God had promised each and every one.

There must have been many times during Israel's 430 years in Egypt that the people felt as if the promises of God would never come true. The Egyptians were so strong that it seemed very foolish indeed to expect deliverance. But as the Israelites now carried the bones of Joseph along, they could not help but say: 'Joseph was right all along. He said God would visit us and deliver us, and it is all coming true.'

We also have promises from God. One of these is that the Lord Jesus will finally return to take his people home. The dead in Christ shall rise first, and those who are alive will be caught up to meet the Lord in the air (1 Thess. 4:13-18).

Scepticism abounds today. Many modern Pharaohs are quick to assure us that we are fools to believe such a promise. It was given such a long time ago that it should be obvious to all that it cannot possibly come true!

The bones of Joseph speak to us. They tell us that it doesn't matter how huge the odds are and how many years pass, God will eventually keep all of his promises, including those about Christ's return and the resurrection of his people. Yes, those promises will come true, and because they are sure, all believers can triumphantly say:

> Mine eyes shall see him in that day,
> The God who died for me,
> And all my rising bones shall say,

Lord, who is like to thee?[1]

When those promises are finally fulfilled, we, the people of God, will take as our own the ancient words of Joshua: 'Not a word failed of any good thing which the Lord had spoken ... All came to pass' (Josh. 21:45, see also Josh. 23:14).

The words of our text yield yet another important truth, that is,

God is sufficient for his people

We glean this truth from these words: 'And the Lord went before them by day in a pillar of cloud to lead the way, and by night in a pillar of fire to give them light, so as to go by day and night. He did not take away the pillar of cloud by day or the pillar of fire by night from before the people' (vv.21-22).

The pillar of cloud by day and the pillar of fire by night were visible tokens of God's presence with his people and means by which he led them along. The cloud also gave them shade by day, and the fire gave them light by night.

God is still present with his people and still sufficient for their every need. And the Lord still leads his people along.

While we are not travelling through an actual physical wilderness as were the people of Israel, we are indeed in a wilderness. This world is very much a spiritual wilderness. It poses all sorts of hardships and difficulties for us as we journey along. The hardships are so many and the difficulties so imposing that it often appears as if God is nowhere near, that he is not protecting us and he is not leading us. And Satan is ever near to assure us that God is not near.

We must learn to resist the devil. And when he points to our circumstances and urges us to draw certain evil conclusions about God, we must cling to the promises of God and say on the basis of those promises: 'God is near when he does not seem to be, he protects us when we do not sense it, and he leads us even when we seem to wander aimlessly.'

All of this will become abundantly clear when the journey is finally over and faith gives way to sight. Until then we must be satisfied to see with the eye of faith. Faith does not see everything, but what it sees is real and true.

11 | The crossing of the Red Sea

Exodus 14:10-31

These verses bring us to one of the best known miracles in the Bible. I propose that we study it by first reviewing the historical events and then exploring something of the spiritual significance.

The historical events

The people of Israel were on their way out of Egypt, but Moses was not leading them by the shortest route to Canaan. Instead he led them into what appeared to be a dead end.

As the multitude of Israelites made camp beside the Red Sea (v.2), there may very well have been a good deal of discussion about the route Moses would take to get them around the sea.

That which began as a topic of idle conversation suddenly became critically important. As the people camped beside the sea, they looked behind them to see the army of Pharaoh furiously descending upon them (v.10). They immediately realized that Pharaoh had experienced a change of heart and had mustered his forces to either take them back to cruel bondage or to kill them (v.12).

With the Red Sea before them and Pharaoh's army behind them, it is not surprising to read that the Israelites were 'very afraid' (v.10). It is always good to cry out to the Lord in times of distress, and that is exactly what the people of Israel did (v.10).

But the faith that caused them to seek God was mixed with a good measure of unbelief and doubt. We are told that the people also complained to Moses (vv.11-12). Here we get a glimpse into the burden and heartache of leadership. God's people can often be very hard on their spiritual leaders.

Their complaining is almost comical. It came on the heels of the ten plagues which God had unleashed on Egypt, all of which made it indisputably clear that Pharaoh was no match for God.

It was absurd for another reason. Did it make sense for God to bring them this far only to let them perish?

Faith often gets a helping hand from common sense, but both faith and common sense were in short supply on this occasion.

The people may have been in a panic, but God wasn't. There is no panic button in heaven. And what appears to us to be a dead end is nothing more than an open door for God.

What the people of Israel may have been regarding as incompetence on the part of Moses was far from it. They did not realize that they were in this predicament because God planned it this way. Their difficulty was designed to bring glory to God, to bring just judgement on Pharaoh and his army, and to confirm and solidify the people in their faith.

God always knows what he is about, and even when it appears that he doesn't know what he is doing, we may rest assured that he does.

Our responsibility – and privilege! – is to simply trust God even when we don't understand what he is doing.

While the flame of faith was flickering in the people, it was burning brightly in Moses. He encouraged his people with these words: 'Do not be afraid. Stand still, and see the salvation of the Lord, which He will accomplish for you today. For the Egyptians whom you see today, you shall see again no more forever. The Lord will fight for you, and you shall hold your peace' (vv.13-14).

And fight for Israel is exactly what the Lord did. He commanded Moses to lift his rod over the sea (v.16), and he promised that the sea would open as the people went forward (v.15). Moses did as the Lord commanded. The sea opened as the people moved forward. With a wall of water on each side and with the ground under their feet being dry, the Israelites were able to get safely across. When the army of Egypt attempted to follow, Moses again stretched his rod over the sea, and those walls of water came tumbling down to drown the Egyptians (vv.21-30).

The people of Israel were saved, and the enemy was destroyed (vv.21-30).

The spiritual significance

The personal level

This passage certainly speaks to us on a personal level. It may be that you are confronting a set of circumstances that seem to be too much for you, and there seems to be no way of escape. You can take consolation in knowing that the same God who was sufficient for Israel on that occasion will prove to be sufficient for you.

The redemptive level

But we must resist the tendency to look at Old Testament passages only through the lens of ourselves as individuals. In other words, we must constantly remind ourselves that the Bible is a book of redemption, and all its passages, including those in the Old Testament, have some connection with that theme.

We might say God gave a preview of all of human history when he spoke these words to Satan in the garden of Eden:

> *And I will put enmity*
> *Between you and the woman,*
> *And between your seed and*
> *her Seed;*
> *He shall bruise your head,*
> *And you shall bruise His heel* (Gen. 3:15)

We can understand history only if we keep those words in mind. Behind the human realm is the conflict between Satan and the seed of the woman, that is, Christ. This conflict also exists between Satan's seed – his people – and the seed or people of Christ.

In light of this, we can say that the Egyptians' enslavement of the people of Israel was nothing less than Satan launching an all-out assault on the people and the promises of God. It was his way of keeping the people of Israel out of the land of Canaan, the land to which the Messiah was to come.

This led Jonathan Edwards to say: 'Hell was as much, nay more engaged in that affair than Egypt was. The pride and cruelty of Satan, that old serpent, was more concerned in it than Pharaoh's.'1

But Satan, powerful and clever as he is, can never overthrow God or thwart his purposes.

God's triumph over Pharaoh and his army was nothing less than a triumph over Satan and all his evil hosts. Furthermore, it was a preview of an even greater triumph, that is, the one that the Lord Jesus Christ achieved when he died on the cross. That triumph enabled the apostle Paul to write of Christ: 'Having disarmed principalities and powers, He made a public spectacle of them, triumphing over them in it' (Col. 2:15).

The people of Israel viewed their situation as hopeless. They were caught in what appeared to be an inescapable vice with the Red Sea in front of them and Pharaoh behind them. But God's wisdom and power made a way of escape.

The situation must have appeared equally hopeless to the disciples of Jesus who saw him crucified. They believed him to be the Messiah, but there he was hanging on a Roman cross. And Satan and all his hellions must have danced with glee as they saw him hanging there. To their minds a crucified Messiah was a failed Messiah.

But the same wisdom and power that was at work at the Red Sea was at work on that cross. And just as that wisdom and power opened a way for the people of Israel to escape, so God's wisdom and power opened the way of eternal salvation for all those who believe.

Satan could never have guessed the genius of that cross. The death Jesus died there did not signal his defeat as Satan supposed. It was a special kind of death, a death in which Jesus received the wrath of God instead of sinners. In receiving that wrath himself, the Lord Jesus freed them from receiving it and, in doing so, freed them from Satan's dominion.

We might say the Lord Jesus Christ inflicted a bruise on Satan's head at the Red Sea, but he crushed his head on the cross.

This passage does more, however, than picture God's provision of eternal salvation. It also shows us the way to receive this salvation. This way can be found in the words Moses spoke to his people: 'Stand still, and see the salvation of the Lord, ... The Lord will fight for you, and you shall hold your peace' (vv.13-14).

There are indeed things for us to do after we are saved, but there is absolutely nothing we can do until we are saved. We must say with the hymn-writer:

> *Nothing in my hand I bring,*
> *Simply to Thy cross I cling*

Those who rest on the finished work of the Lord Jesus Christ will be able to find yet another parallel between themselves and the Israelites of old. Just as those people all made it through the Red Sea and safely on the other side, so those who trust Christ will make it safely to the eternal shore where Satan and all his Pharaohs will never be able to afflict them again.

12 | Three songs of praise

Exodus 15:1-21

The first fourteen chapters of Exodus contain many surprises. A bush burns but is not consumed. Plague after plague fall upon Egypt. The Red Sea parts before the people of Israel, and they cross on dry land.

The verses before us contain no surprises. They relate the songs of praise of Moses, Miriam and the people of Israel after their miraculous crossing of the Red Sea. These are songs of praise – the first songs in the Bible. It is, I say, not surprising that the people should express praise to God for what he had done for them. It would have been astonishing had they not.

The last verse of chapter fourteen says: 'Thus Israel saw the great work which the Lord had done in Egypt.' And chapter fifteen opens: 'Then Moses and the children of Israel sang this song to the Lord.'

Yes, of course!

Let us turn our attention, then, to the song of Moses (vv.1-19) and the song of Miriam (vv.20-21). This may very well seem to be a pointless endeavour if we do not keep in mind that the historical event celebrated in these songs has tremendous spiritual value and significance for us.

The song of Moses and the people (vv.1-19)

This song consists of two parts. First it celebrates...

What the Lord had done (vv.1-12)

And what had he done? He had 'triumphed gloriously' by throwing both 'The horse and its rider into the sea' (v.2).

The Lord could do this because he is 'a man of war' who has strength (v.2) and power (v.6). The word 'thrown' (v.1) suggests hurling something with great force.

The strength of the Lord is such that the greatest strength men can muster cannot compare. Many of that time may very well have selected Pharaoh and his army as the strongest force imaginable. Pharaoh himself was quite confident of his own strength, saying:

> I will pursue,
> I will overtake,
> I will divide the spoil;
> My desire shall be satisfied on
> them.
> I will draw my sword,
> My hand shall destroy them (v.9)

How did the Lord respond to such strength? 'The blast of his nostrils' was all that was necessary bring Pharaoh's strength to nothing (v.8). When the tower-builders of Babel set out they said: 'Come, let us build ourselves a city, and a tower whose top is in the heavens; ...' (Gen. 11:4). Their tower would show their tremendous strength! But that same tower was so infinitesimal to God that he had to come down to see it! (Gen. 11:5).

Such a God is in his own class or category. There are other things that men call 'gods,' but only the God whom the Israelites praised is worthy of the name:

> Who is like You, O Lord, among the gods?
> Who is like You, glorious in holiness,
> Fearful in praises, doing wonders (v.11)

Having celebrated what the Lord had done, the song moves to celebrating

What he would do (vv.13-19)

Moses and his people, as it were, lifted their eyes to look beyond the triumph of God over Pharaoh to see an even larger triumph ahead, namely, the triumph of God over the inhabitants of Canaan, all of whom would 'melt away' (v.15) before this same glorious God.

In fact, the news of Israel's crossing of the Red Sea would travel to these people and cause them to experience sorrow (v.14), dismay (v.15), trembling (v.15), fear (v.16) and dread (v.16).

This triumph was so certain that the Israelites could sing as if it were already accomplished. And this they did by saying:

> You in Your mercy have led forth
> The people whom You have redeemed;
> You have guided them in Your strength
> To Your holy habitation (v.13)

It often seems that the people of God today are the ones who are experiencing fear and dread. The evil of our day is so very strong and militant, and the cause of God so often appears to be weak and failing.

If we find ourselves inclined to view things in this way, we need only to remind ourselves of how bleak the situation looked for the Israelites before God sent Moses. How quickly things turned!

On the basis of their experience alone, we can say that when it appears that God is failing, it is in appearance only.

Moses and the people of Israel concluded their song in a most appropriate way, that is, by celebrating the truth of God's unending reign (v.18). Matthew Henry says of the Israelites: 'They had now seen an end of Pharaoh's reign; but time itself shall not put a period to Jehovah's reign, which, like himself, is eternal, and not subject to change.'[1]

The song of Miriam and the women (vv.20-21)

After Moses led 'the children of Israel' (v.1) in praise, Miriam did the same with 'all the women' (v.20).

Miriam is here called 'the prophetess' (v.20). This has caused some to wonder how this can be reconciled with the teachings of the apostle Paul (1 Tim. 2:12). But the fact that Miriam led only the women in praise to God plainly places her action outside the purview of the apostle's teaching.

While the issue of female leadership is certainly important, to focus on it here is to move from what this passage itself emphasizes, that is, praise to God.

By opening the Red Sea, he Lord had delivered both the men and women of Israel from the Egyptians. It was fitting, therefore, for the women to join in the praise. They did so by dancing, playing 'timbrels' or tambourines and by singing words similar to those with which the song of Moses begins:

> *Sing to the Lord,*
> *For He has triumphed gloriously!*
> *The horse and its rider*
> *He has thrown into the sea!* (v.21)

The dancing, playing and singing make it obvious that the praise of the women was invested with great feeling. This was not half-spirited, faint praise from cold, tepid hearts. It was robust praise from full hearts.

As such it challenges us to carefully consider and evaluate our praise. The deliverance of Israel from Egypt was certainly no small matter, but it pales in comparison to the deliverance Christians enjoy through Christ – deliverance from sin and judgement. Do our worship services give others the impression that we have indeed experienced a great deliverance?

The song of the redeemed of all ages

The songs of Moses and Miriam point us ahead to that time when all who have experienced that greater deliverance will gather by another sea, the 'sea of glass' (Rev. 15:2), and 'sing the song of Moses, the servant of God, and the song of the Lamb, saying:

> *Great and marvelous are Your works,*
> *Lord God Almighty!*
> *Just and true are Your ways,*
> *O King of the saints!*
> *Who shall not fear You, O*
> *Lord, and glorify Your name?*

For You alone are holy.
For all nations shall come and
worship before You,
For Your judgments have been
manifested (Rev. 15:3b-4)

This is called at one and the same time 'the song of Moses' and the song of the Lamb' because, in the words of Geoffrey Wilson, 'the deliverance God wrought through his servant Moses foreshadowed that which he wrought through the Lamb. The continuity of God's saving purpose in both dispensations means that the Old Testament phrases which make up the hymn can be applied to the greater exodus which he accomplished through Christ ... .'[2]

Richard Brooks encourages us to be looking forward ' ... to that glorious day when, delivered from sin and oppression, delivered from the enemy who is always on our tail, and set free in heaven to glorify the God of our salvation, we shall be able to sing this song together as he have never sung it before.'[3]

13 | When you arrive at Marah

Exodus 15:22-26

A song of triumph filled the air as the people of Israel looked upon the Red Sea where Pharaoh and his army had drowned (15:1-21). Hallelujahs abounded.

The people may very well have thought that the rest of their journey would be a snap. They were in for a shock. First, it was the wilderness. For three days they journeyed in the Wilderness of Shur, vainly searching for water (v.22).

Then it was Marah. Moses may very well have sent a team of scouts ahead to find water. Imagine them excitedly returning to announce 'There is water just ahead!'

See the weary travellers summoning strength and quickening their pace as they think about the cool, refreshing springs!

Now listen to these sad words: ' ... when they came to Marah, they could not drink the waters of Marah, for they were bitter. Therefore the name of it was called Marah' (v.23).

Each one of us knows about Marah. As we look upon our respective journeys, we can each point to a time and say: 'I named that place Marah.' We may very well have done the same with many experiences.

Marah means 'bitter.' It is the place of unfulfilled dreams, the place of disappointment. Every time you expected to lift the cup of life to your lips to drink deeply from its pleasures and comforts only to find a bitter taste, you came to Marah.

What have you experienced that has made life bitter? What has robbed you of joy and comfort? Sickness can do it. So can the loss of a loved one, financial reversal, the rebellion of children, the fracture of a friendship, turmoil in society, and, yes, turmoil in the church.

We all come to Marah sooner or later. We all come to that time when life is more bitter than sweet, and our songs of triumph and jubilation turn to laments of woe and despair.

It is not a matter of whether we will come to Marah. It is rather when we will come to it and how we will cope with it. The passage before us provides some help for dealing with the Marahs of life.

The first truth for us to glean from this passage is this:

We must not let the fact that we are in Marah cause Marah to get into us

The people of Israel undoubtedly regarded it as a calamity of the first order that they were in Marah. But the real calamity here is that they allowed Marah to get into them. They should not have allowed their bitter circumstances to make them bitter. But listen to them murmuring against Moses, saying: 'What shall we drink?' (v.24).

We cannot always control our circumstances, but we can and must control ourselves in the midst of our circumstances.

We all know how very hard it is to do this, and we know how very easy it is to become bitter over our circumstances and to take that bitterness out on those around us. How eager we are to do this! We often spread the gospel as if we were dragging a ball and chain. How easy it is to spread discontent as if we had winged feet!

Marah gets into all of us from time to time, but we must not let it settle there. If we do so, we will become known for bitterness. We should all desire to live in such a way that when we die we are known for something of a positive nature.

What an unspeakable tragedy it is for a Christian to live in such a way that when he dies it is said: 'He never got out of Marah' or more accurately: 'He never got Marah out of himself.'

Marah is a bad enough place to visit. It is worse to live there.

A second truth which this passage yields is most cheering:

God is present in Marah and is sufficient for it

How very thankful we should be for these words regarding Moses: 'So he cried out to the Lord, and the Lord showed him a tree' (v.25)!

When the people of Israel journeyed to Marah, they had not journeyed beyond God. Moses sought the Lord and found him – right there in Marah! The Lord is present with his people in the midst of their most heart-wrenching trials, and he is present even when he appears not to be.

The Lord's solution for the bitter waters of Marah seemed to be utterly absurd. Moses was to cast the wood of a tree into those waters. Moses could have argued that such a strategy did not make sense and would be of no avail, but he did as he was told, and the waters were made sweet.

It is interesting that the tree was there all along. God simply had to show it to Moses. We have a tendency to look for a new formula or a secret when life turns bitter. But the cure for our bitter experiences is not something new or different. It is rather something that has been there all along. Because the Lord Jesus Christ hanged on Calvary's tree, he is the believer's tree of life.

By looking to him and his redeeming death, the believer can always find comfort in the bitterness of life. How does this help us? It reminds us that the Lord Jesus Christ experienced bitterness for us of an indescribable nature – the bitterness of the cup of God's wrath. If he were willing to experience the greatest kind of bitterness for us, we should be willing to experience lesser kinds for him.

What a powerful application we can find here for the unbeliever! There is nothing more bitter than the wrath of God, and that bitterness will be experienced by all who do not receive Jesus Christ as Lord and Saviour. If the sinner would escape that wrath, he must look to the 'tree' where Jesus died (Acts 5:30; Gal 3:13; 1 Peter 2:24).

Jesus died there for the express purpose of receiving the wrath of God in the stead of sinners. Unbelieving friend, you may rest assured that on the day of judgement, God's wrath will either be found on Jesus or on you. The only way God's wrath against you will be found on Jesus is by trusting what he did on the cross. Look to the tree!

A final truth for us to glean from this passage is this:

God has a purpose for Marah

God was not taken by surprise by Marah. There were no computer 'foul-ups' in heaven. God did not call in his angels for a severe tongue-lashing: 'Who messed up? The waters of Marah were supposed to be pure!'

No, the people were at Marah because God led them there. Why would God do such a thing? Do we not have the answer in that which we have already noticed? We have established the sufficiency of God for his people. He was sufficient for the bitter waters of Marah. He transformed them into pure, drinkable waters.

Is it not safe to say, therefore, that God's purpose in all this was to bring his people to trust more in his sufficiency? Can we not say that the Lord used the experience at Marah to cast the people more completely upon him and to teach them more fully his sufficiency?

The Lord himself seems to have indicated as much: 'If you diligently heed the voice of the Lord your God and do what is right in His sight, give ear to His commandments and keep all His statutes, I will put none of the diseases on you which I have brought on the Egyptians. For I am the Lord who heals you' (v.26).

No, the Lord was not promising that they would never have so much as a case of the 'sniffles'. Michael Bentley writes: 'It is clear from their subsequent history that God was not promising to heal them of every disease that might possibly befall them. If this was the case, then none of them would ever have died. Nor was he promising to heal them without the use of natural means; he had, after all, used a piece of wood to heal the bitter waters of Marah. What he did promise them was this: he would not bring on them any of the diseases he had brought upon the Egyptians.'[1]

The diseases he had brought on the Egyptians were, of course, the plagues. The promise he is now giving to the Israelites is that they were be healed, that is, preserved or spared, from such plagues if they would walk in obedience to him. On the other hand, failure to obey would indeed result in them experiencing plagues similar to those experienced by the Egyptians (Deut. 28:27). If they chose to live like the Egyptians, they must endure the plagues of the Egyptians.

There is, then, no basis for taking God's promise to the Israelites as a carte blanche guarantee of healing for the sicknesses that come to Christians in the course of living in a world that is characterized by such. To use the promise in this way, as the Charismatic movement seeks to do, makes as much sense as asserting that Christians should never have to buy new clothes because of what God said to Israel in Deuteronomy 29:5.

We must notice that this particular promise was based on their obedience. God's purpose in Marah was, then, to drive home to their hearts a crucial truth: God's people can expect to experience the grace of God in their trials to the degree that they live in obedience to him. The apostle Paul puts it in these words: 'He who sows sparingly will also reap sparingly, and he who bountifully will also reap bountifully. . . . And God is able to make all grace abound toward you, that you, always having all sufficiency in all things, may have an abundance for every good work' (2 Cor. 9:6,8).

If we want God's sufficiency to flow into the Marahs of our lives, we must keep the channel of that sufficiency free from the debris of sin. We are told that the Lord's purpose in Marah was to establish a statute and an ordinance for Israel (v.25). S.G. DeGraaf notes: 'The statute was that He would provide for the people in all their needs, and the ordinance was that they would rely on Him.'[2]

14 | Manna from heaven

Exodus 16

This chapter brings us to another of the most striking events in the Old Testament, that is, God giving manna to the people of Israel.

We are looking at this passage because of its abiding value. The truth is God's gift of manna to Israel of old has a lot to do with us.

Henry Law, a preacher in England in the early 1800's, put it this way: 'Manna has many tongues.'[1]

I suggest, therefore, that we listen to the manna of old to see what it has to say to us.

First, it speaks to us about...

The grace of God

How that grace glistens in this passage! Here the Israelites are murmuring – again! The cause of their unhappiness this time was that they were not eating as well in the wilderness as they had in Egypt (vv.2-3).

This murmuring had a very sharp edge to it. They said to Moses and Aaron: ' ... you have brought us out into this wilderness to kill this whole assembly with hunger' (v.3).

We again have to marvel at the lack of common sense evidenced by those words. Would God have rained plagues upon Egypt and opened the Red Sea so he could starve his people?

The Lord would have been justified in killing the people on the spot, but he said to Moses: 'Behold, I will rain bread from heaven for you' (v.4).

There is a lesson here for us. We are no more worthy of God and his blessings than those people. If God were to give us what we deserve, we would perish. But God, who could rain nothing but judgement upon us, chooses to rain many blessings instead. How good and gracious he is!

God's regard for faith

Let's listen to the manna again. It also speaks to us about God's regard for faith.

Look again at what the Lord said to Moses: 'Behold, I will rain bread from heaven for you. And the people shall go out and gather a certain quota every day, that I may test them, whether they will walk in My law or not' (v.4).

Yes, the Lord sent the manna to supply the need of Israel, but he also sent it to test them. That was a part of his purpose in doing so.

God could have sent enough manna to last for weeks, months and even years. There is never any need to put limits on the power of God. But God gave them the manna on a daily basis. It fell during the night, and they were responsible to collect it in the morning. The only exception to this was on the seventh day, the Sabbath. The manna would not fall on the night preceding that day. The people would, therefore, have to collect enough on the previous day to last them through the Sabbath (vv.22-30).

God ordained the manna, therefore, to test their faith. Would they trust God to send it each night? Would they trust him to send enough to carry them through the Sabbath?

The passage tells us that many of the people failed the test. Some of them tried to save enough manna for the next day (vv.19-20). And some went out on the Sabbath to gather it (v.27).

What is there here for us? Are we not to conclude that we are to look to the Lord each and every day for the grace sufficient for us? The Lord does not give us in one gigantic bestowment the grace and strength we need for all of life. He gives these in daily portions, and he expects us to trust him for them.

How God prizes faith in his children! And how grieved he is by our lack of faith!

Christ

Incline your ear to the manna once again. Can you not hear it saying something else? Listen carefully and you will hear it speaking the name of the Lord Jesus Christ.

I do not hesitate to say that another part of God's purpose in sending the manna was to point his people to the Lord Jesus. We draw this conclusion on the basis of what Jesus himself said: 'Your fathers ate the manna in the wilderness, and are dead . . . . I am the living bread which comes down from heaven' (John 6:49, 51a).

How did that ancient manna typify the Lord Jesus? Here are some answers:

+ as the manna was sent from heaven, so was Jesus.

+ as the manna was mysterious (v.15), so the Lord Jesus and his salvation are beyond human comprehension.

+ as the manna was small and unimpressive in appearance, so was Jesus in his humanity.

+ as the manna was a gift, not created by human toil, so it is with Jesus and the salvation he came to provide.

+ as the manna was for every Israelite of every state and age, so Christ is the Saviour for those of every state and age.

+ as the manna was pleasant to the taste and satisfying to the appetite, so the Lord Jesus is pleasant and satisfying. (Everyone who has come to know him has found him to be sweet to the taste and satisfying to the soul).

+ as the manna had to be personally appropriated by the Israelites, so Christ must be personally and individually appropriated by faith.

+ as the manna was sufficient for the people all through their wilderness journeyings, so the Lord Jesus Christ is sufficient for his people all through their pilgrim journey in this world.

✦ as the 'mixed multitude' (unbelievers) in Israel despised the manna (Num. 11:4-6), so Christ is despised by unbelievers today.

Such parallels caused Henry Law to write: 'When the whole family of man, in Adam's loins, stood before God, lost, ruined and undone – one leprous mass of misery and sin – shameless, tearless, prayerless – mercy took up the song, and promised that a Saviour should descend, even an incarnate God. Reader, your heart is rock indeed, if you hear this, and give no praises to Jehovah's grace.'[2]

No type of Christ is perfect. We must say, therefore, that while the manna prefigured the Lord Jesus in some ways, it falls short in other ways:

✦ the manna was physical food while Christ is spiritual food, food for the internal man.

✦ the manna decayed when kept, the Lord Jesus never decays.

✦ the manna was found only in the morning, but the Lord Jesus can be found at any time.

✦ the manna ceased when the people of Israel entered Canaan, but Christ will continue to be the manna on which his people feed throughout eternity.

It is not enough, however, to say that Christ is the manna for the Christian. We must also think about where the believer finds this manna. In other words, how does the believer feed on Christ? The answer is by looking into the Word of God where the Lord Jesus Christ is set forth.

Every Christian should take up the Word of God each morning so he or she can feed on the Lord Jesus Christ. We might go so far as to say that it is as we feed on the manna of the Word that we feed on the manna of the Lord Jesus himself.

Testimony

If we listen to the manna yet again, we will hear it utter the word 'testimony.'

Verse 32 tells us that the Lord commanded that 'an omer' be filled with manna and kept for future generations 'that they may see the bread' with which God fed their forefathers.

Verse 34 tells us Aaron laid the omer of manna 'before the Testimony.'

The Testimony refers to the law of God that was kept in the tabernacle. It is called the Testimony because it is God testifying of his own holy character.

The tabernacle had not yet been built when the manna was given, but Moses, writing later, is simply telling us that God's commandment regarding the manna was kept when the tabernacle was finished.

The fact that the pot of manna was to be kept before the Testimony was itself a testimony to future generations about God's gracious and faithful care for his people.

As we read the account of the manna, we are reminded that God has been gracious and faithful to us. We can show that we are profoundly grateful to God for his care by telling others about it, especially our own children.

15 | God's provision for undeserving people

Exodus 17:1-7

We never advance so far spiritually that we advance beyond sin. The people of Israel should by this time have been far advanced spiritually. They had been the recipients of mighty supplies of the grace of God. The Lord had convinced Pharaoh to let them go by raining plague after plague upon Egypt. The Lord had opened the Red Sea so they, his people, could pass safely over. The Lord had purified the waters of Marah so they could drink. The Lord had supplied manna in the wilderness.

But all of these things seem to have made little or no impression upon these people. Here we find them facing another challenge, and here we find them grumbling again!

This passage tells us that they journeyed 'according to the commandment of the Lord and camped in Rephidim; but there was no water for the people to drink' (v.1).

We must not disconnect the things that this passage links together: they were led by the Lord to a place where there was no water.

We would like to believe that if we are living for the Lord and walking with him, we will not come into difficulties. This passage makes it clear that the Lord often leads his people into hardships. We may rest assured that he has a good and benevolent purpose for doing so.

In light of what we have noted above – all the things God had done on behalf of his people – we might expect to read that they shouted 'Hallelujah!' when they came upon this new crisis. We could certainly understand them doing so. Each of their previous crises had given them opportunity to view the grace and power of their God. Why did they expect it to be any different with this one? Should they not have said one to another: 'I can hardly wait to see what God is going to do now!'

But they did nothing of the sort. Instead they 'contended with Moses' (v.2) to the point that he cried out to God: 'What shall I do with this people? They are almost ready to stone me!' (v.4).

These people were amazing. They ended up being humiliated and embarrassed each time they grumbled, but they kept right on grumbling!

God responded to this episode of murmuring by once again being gracious to them. God loves to magnify his grace!

How hard it is for us to comprehend the grace of God! It is not at all uncommon to hear someone say: 'God must have seen something in us, or he would not have saved us.'

But there is never anything in us to prompt the grace of God. The marvel is that God saves his people even though there is absolutely nothing at all to commend them. Someone has rightly observed: 'Two things man has never fathomed – the depth of sin and the grace of God.'[1]

This particular instalment of the grace of God came in a very unusual way. God commanded Moses to use his rod to strike a rock in the presence of the elders of Israel (v.5), and he promised to send water from that rock to quench the thirst of the people (v.6).

Some flatly deny that such a thing could happen. Others try to find a natural way to explain it. But those who believe in the God of the Bible have no difficulty here. The God who made all things, including rocks and water, has no trouble releasing the latter from the former!

What are we to gain from this account? The overarching lesson here is clear, and it is a happy lesson indeed – our God is a providing God. This truth is manifested in both the temporal realms and the spiritual realm.

God provides for his people temporally

God supplies his people with the necessities of life. We must be clear on this. God has not promised to supply our greeds but rather our needs. There may very well be things we think are needful that God views otherwise.

And we must not take this principle to mean that we do not need to take appropriate measures to take care of ourselves. God does not promise to supply the needs of a person who is too lazy to work.

With those things in place, we can confidently pray as the Lord Jesus taught us: 'Give us this day our daily bread' (Matt. 6:11). And we can lay hold with confidence of the promise of the apostle Paul: ' ... my God shall supply all your need according to His riches in glory by Christ Jesus' (Phil. 4:19).

How faithful God has been to us in this area of our temporal needs!

God supplies for his people spiritually

What a fascinating and riveting picture we have here of the gospel! We are entitled to regard it in this way because of these words from Paul: 'For they drank of that spiritual Rock that followed them, and that Rock was Christ' (1 Cor. 10:4).

What parallels can we find between the rock that Moses struck and the saving work of the Lord Jesus Christ? Here are some:

- ✦ as the people of Israel would have perished without water, so sinners will perish eternally without salvation.

- ✦ as the rock appeared to be a very unlikely place from which to get water, so the cross of Christ appears to be a very unlikely way for God to provide eternal salvation.

- ✦ as the rock represents might and strength but still yielded water, so the sovereign, mighty Christ still yields saving grace.

- ✦ as Moses had to smite the rock to draw water from it, so the Lord Jesus Christ had to be smitten on the cross in order to provide salvation.

- ✦ as Moses was to smite the rock one time only, so Christ had to die only once (Heb. 9:28) to provide salvation (remember what happened when Moses later smote when he was commanded only to speak! - Numbers 20:1-13).

- ✦ as the water that flowed from the rock was more than sufficient for the people of Israel, so the salvation that flows from Christ's redeeming death is more than sufficient to cover our sins.

✦ as the people of Israel had to personally drink of the water from the rock, so sinners must by faith personally receive the Lord Jesus Christ.

✦ as the Lord Jesus Christ was the rock that followed the people of Israel (1 Cor. 10:4), so Christ continues to walk with his people after he saves them. And he continues to grant them grace and to supply their spiritual needs!

Each of these parallels between the rock and Christ would yield much spiritual benefit if explored in depth. We must be content to look in more detail at only one, that is, the smiting of Christ.

On the cross, Jesus was 'smitten.' This means he was afflicted with sufferings.

Who did this smiting? We might think it was the Roman soldiers who so brutally scourged him. The prophet Isaiah says he was 'Smitten by God, and afflicted' (Isa. 53:4). He further says that 'it pleased the Lord to bruise' Jesus (Isa. 53:10).

We are face to face here with a piercing question: Why would God smite Jesus on the cross? Perfect love has always existed between the three persons of the Trinity. How then could the Father smite the Son?

The answer is, of course, that God smote the Son on the cross because Jesus was there in the capacity of the sin-bearer. He had no sins of his own, but he was there to bear the sins of others (1 Peter 2:24).

The holy God has decreed that the sinner be afflicted with judgement for his sins. That penalty has to be paid before God can set the sinner free. The sinner must either pay it himself or someone must pay it for him. If Jesus was on the cross to pay that penalty, he had to be afflicted with judgement.

While on the cross Jesus cried out 'My God! My God! why have You forsaken Me?' (Matt. 27:46). The reason he did so is because he was there enduring an eternity's worth of separation from God the Father. He was there smitten by God so that believing sinners will never have to be smitten.

I do not hesitate to say, then, that God specifically commanded Moses to smite the rock in the wilderness so he, God, could provide a beautiful picture of the coming death of the Lord Jesus. How grateful we should be for that redeeming death!

Exodus 17:8-16

We cannot remind ourselves too frequently that the Bible does not record historical events just for the sake of history. The history in the Bible has spiritual meaning from which spiritual applications are to be made.

The verses of our text provide us with an excellent example of this point. If all we have here is nothing more than sketchy details of an ancient battle, there is virtually no purpose at all in spending our time on this passage.

But because of the special and unique nature of the Bible, we can say that this battle is recorded so we can look beyond it to issues of momentous importance.

This account serves to remind us of...

The reality of spiritual warfare

'Now Amalek came and fought with Israel in Rephidim' (v.8). This statement will not have much meaning for us until we realize the special nature of the nation of Israel. This nation was like no other. It stood in a special covenant relationship with God. This covenant was originally established with Abraham and passed down to Isaac and Jacob. In selecting Jacob as the bearer of the covenant, God by-passed his brother Esau.

There was, therefore, hostility between Esau and Jacob and between Esau's descendants and Jacob's descendants. The Amalekites were descendants of Amalek, the grandson of Esau, and they held a deep-seated hatred for the people of Israel.

This constitutes a vivid fulfilment of Genesis 3:15. There we are told that the human race would be divided into two parts – those who belong to Satan and those who belong to God. And we are further told that the former would hate and persecute the latter.

The Amalekites' hatred of Israel must be traced, then, to Satan himself.

What does all this have to do with us? That hatred of Satan and his people for God and his people is still in effect. It has not been nullified or cancelled. It is an on-going reality. Henry Law writes: 'Believer, the race of Cain, of Ishmael, of Esau still lives. Be ready. Their hate is sure. Their wily steps are near. When least expected, they will plot their worst.'[1]

Because of this hatred, Satan is constantly attacking the people of God in various ways, and the people of God are compelled to defend themselves against his attacks. To be a Christian is to be engaged in spiritual warfare against Satan and his forces (Eph. 6:10-20).

We would do well to carefully consider a detail about the Amalekites' attack on Israel that is mentioned in the later account in Deuteronomy, namely, that it was launched against the weary Israelites who were straggling along at the rear of the company (Deut. 25:17-18).

Those who are most vulnerable to Satan are those who are lagging behind, those who are not diligent and vigorous in their Christianity. The best defence against Satan is to be strong in our Christian walk, and we can only do this if we adopt the spirit and mentality of a warrior. Henry Law says: 'Heaven's crown sits only on a warrior's brow.'[2]

This passage also gives us insight into...

The way in which we must go about spiritual warfare

Moses adopted a twofold strategy when Amalek attacked. He gave Joshua some men and sent them out to fight, and he stationed himself on a hill over the battlefield (v.9). There he would hold up the rod of God over his soldiers, invoking, as it were, God's blessings on them and reminding them that their God would give them strength to overcome.

What are we to learn from this as we engage in spiritual warfare? Does it not underscore for us the importance of balance in Christian living?

Some Christians lean too heavily on 'the Moses side' or 'the trust side.' They emphasize so much that the battle is the Lord's that they give the impression that there is nothing for the people of God to do.

Others incline too much to 'the Joshua side' or 'the action side.' They emphasize so much the need to be serving the Lord that they neglect the importance of trusting the Lord.

We must remember that God is sovereign over all, and we can completely trust him to help us in our spiritual warfare and to ultimately give us victory. But we must also remember that God in his sovereignty has determined to work through means. We must not be content to sit in idleness. We must be up and about doing the Master's business.

The perfect blend is illustrated for us by the command that Oliver Cromwell gave his soldiers centuries ago: 'Trust God and keep your powder dry.'

Trusting God does not in any way negate the importance of being diligent.

This passage also alerts us to...

Our danger in spiritual warfare

When Moses held up the rod of God, the soldiers of Israel prevailed against Amalek. But when Moses arms grew so tired that he had to lower the rod, Amalek prevailed (v.11).

Every Christian knows about this. We serve the Lord energetically for a while, and then we get 'weary while doing good)' (Gal. 6:9). The flesh is weak. The devil is strong. Our efforts seem to accomplish so little. All of these things – and many more – cause us to grow weary. The incredibly sad thing today is that so many Christians seem to be weary when they have been expending little or no effort!

The reality of weariness in spiritual warfare lays before us the importance of Christians helping each other. Moses was not on the hill alone. Aaron and Hur were there with him, and when he became weary, they seated him on a stone and held up his arms (v.12).

Brothers and sisters in Christ, we are not only responsible to fight Satan and his forces ourselves. We must also help our fellow-believers fight. Are you encouraging anyone? Are you supporting anyone?

Finally, this passage calls to our minds...

The main resource Christians have in their spiritual struggles

What is this resource? We can turn once again to Henry Law for the answer: 'Moses interceding on the hill shows Jesus interceding on the higher heights.'[3]

What a blessed thought! As believers are engaged in their grim battle with Satan, the Lord Jesus himself is engaged on their behalf. He is not sitting in heaven with nothing to do. He did not lay his work down when he returned to heaven. He did not turn it all over to us. He is carrying it on from heaven's glory.

As we struggle in living the Christian life and fighting against Satan, the Lord Jesus Christ asks the Father to provide us strength and grace and wisdom. If it were not for his on-going work, we would be utterly defeated. How little most of us realize these things!

Henry Law rejoiced in this truth with these wonderful words: 'What? Is He still engaged in work? Wondrous tidings! Hear, all who call Him Lord: He ever loves you, and ever labours in your cause. His eye is never turned away. His hands cannot hang down. His heavens are the office-chamber of your soul's concerns.'[4]

Yes, thank God, the hands of Jesus never hang down as Moses' did. Jesus never grows weary in carrying out his work on our behalf. He is sufficient for us today, and he will be sufficient for us tomorrow. Because he is our ever-active and all-sufficient Christ, we can gladly join with the apostle Paul in saying: 'I can do all things through Christ who strengthens me' (Phil. 4:19).

Exodus 18

We have followed Moses from one crisis to another. In each situation we have found God doing something extraordinary.

We might by now have the impression that Moses' life consisted of nothing more than crises and extraordinary happenings.

This chapter indicates otherwise. Here we descend from the mountain of the extraordinary to walk for a while on the plain of the ordinary. We should not complain about the ordinariness of life. It can be a wonderful thing.

Here Moses receives a visit from his father-in-law, his wife and his two sons (v.6). What is more ordinary than a visit from relatives?

By the way, we assume that Moses' wife and sons stayed with him from this point forward. This is indicated by verse 27 which only mentions his father-in-law departing.

A visit from a father-in-law may seem to be so ordinary that we find ourselves wondering why this account is in the Bible. I answer by saying that this ordinary visit accomplished some extraordinary things. Moses and Jethro used their time together to talk about some very important issues and to help each other. Their talk was not just about gardening, golfing and the weather.

Let us look, then, at how Moses helped his father-in-law and how his father-in-law helped him.

Moses helps Jethro find the Lord (vv.8-12)

This chapter begins by telling us that Jethro was 'the priest of Midian.' This piece of information, along with what we are about to see, indicates that

Jethro was not yet a believer in the God of Moses. He was rather a priest in a pagan religion.

We often fritter away opportunities to speak to our family members about the Lord. In these days of political correctness and tolerance, many Christians find themselves very reluctant to speak about their faith at all. Afraid that they will be accused of 'imposing' their religion on someone else, they keep quiet. We have witnessed in the last several years a concerted effort to keep Christians silent, and many Christians seem quite content to comply.

By the way, attempts to silence any other groups would be met, as they should, with scorn. But the same media that heap ridicule on attempts to silence other groups rarely speak out against silencing Christians.

A recent cartoon showed a man arriving at the entrance of heaven only to see this sign: 'Welcome to heaven. Keep your religion to yourself.' Noting the newcomer's surprise, the attendant at the gate said: 'That's the reason it is so peaceful around here.'

But Moses did not keep his religion to himself. He 'told his father-in-law all that the Lord had done ... and how the Lord had delivered them' (v.8).

We who know the Lord have not seen the things that Moses saw – the burning bush, the plagues, the opening of the Red Sea, the miraculous supplies of food and water in the wilderness – but we can still speak of all that the Lord has done and how he has delivered us. We can speak about the reality and guilt of our sin, our awareness of coming judgement and our consequent feeling of hopelessness and despair.

We can proceed to talk about how we came to have peace and rest in our souls by believing in the gospel message of a crucified and risen Saviour.

We must never let the fact that we have not seen miracles such as Moses saw obscure the fact that we have experienced the most staggering of all, that is, God forgiving our sins and saving our souls.

When Jethro heard what Moses had to say, he, Jethro, 'rejoiced for all the good which the Lord had done for Israel' and said 'Blessed be the Lord, who has delivered you ...' (vv.9,10).

Jethro was not through. He proceeded to speak these telling words: 'Now I know that the Lord is greater than all the gods; ...' (v.11).

This constitutes a genuine confession of faith. The words of Moses were effectively used by the Spirit of God to drive this truth home to Jethro's heart – Moses' God was the only true God. That meant the gods Jethro had been serving were false gods. The only reasonable course of action, therefore, was for him to abandon his false gods to embrace with true and living faith the one true God.

All true conversion consists of breaking with our false gods and false beliefs and resting completely on the God who has provided deliverance for sinners through the redeeming death of his Son, Jesus Christ.

Jethro gave evidence of his new faith by giving 'a burnt offering and sacrifices to God' (v.12). The sacrifices of the Old Testament were designed, of course, to point to the sacrifice that the Lord Jesus Christ would make on the cross. Since that sacrifice has been made, there is now no need for animal sacrifices. But everyone who is truly saved by the grace of God will most certainly be trying to offer himself as a living sacrifice to God (Rom. 12:1) as well as the sacrifice of praise to God (Heb. 13:15).

Whether we look in the Old Testament or New, we cannot find a conversion which did not lead to a changed life. Away then with this modern teaching that suggests that one can truly be saved and have no interest in the things of God!

Jethro helps Moses serve the Lord (vv.13-27)

Moses did the best thing for Jethro that anyone can do for another. He shared with him the truth about God. As Jethro received that truth, he undoubtedly longed for some way to demonstrate his gratitude for what Moses had done.

He found that way the very next day as he noticed Moses devoting the whole day to handling the conflicts and problems of the people (vv.13-16).

After witnessing this, Jethro spoke these wise words to Moses: 'The thing that you do is not good. Both you and these people who are with you will surely wear yourselves out. For this thing is too much for you; you are not able to perform it by yourself' (vv.17b-18).

Jethro also had a proposal ready at hand. He suggested that Moses learn the art of delegation. He was to select able men to carry out the work that he had been doing (vv.21-23).

The advice Jethro gave Moses is as valuable for us as it was for Moses. It leads us to the following applications:

> ◆ As Jethro took an immediate interest in the people of Israel, so new believers in Christ will take an interest in the church.

> ◆ Even the best leaders need spiritual counsel and advice. No one knows everything about the ways of the Lord and the work of the Lord.

> ◆ The church works best when the pastor focuses his time and energy on his main tasks (the ministry of the Word and prayer - Acts 6:2) and leaves other tasks to the people.

> ◆ The work of the church cannot properly be carried out if the people doing it are not the right type of people. We should notice that Jethro suggested that Moses find 'able men' who had spiritual qualities (v.21). It is one thing to agree that pastors should not try to do all the work. It is quite another thing to be willing to pay the price to be the type of person who can help do the work.

This is, then, a happy passage of Scripture. It presents us with two men who help each other. Moses helped Jethro find the Lord, and Jethro helped Moses serve the Lord.

The main thing this chapter wants us to carry away is the importance of helping those around us. Are you doing so? Look around. There is someone near you who needs to know the Lord. Are you sharing the message of the gospel? Look around again. There is someone around you who needs encouragement and help in his service to the Lord. What are you doing to provide that encouragement and help?

18 | Covenant and Mediator

Exodus 19:1-25

When we come to this chapter, we stand on the brink of some most important developments. This is the first in a series of chapters that deal with God constituting the people of Israel into a nation and entering into a covenant relationship with them. This was accomplished at Mt. Sinai (vv.1-2), which is also known as Mt. Horeb. This is the same place where Moses was called to lead Israel out of bondage (3:1). Centuries later Elijah would go to this mountain in deep despondency (1 Kings 19:8).

We will not see the importance of these chapters if we assume that they only pertain to the people of ancient Israel. The truths unfolded here have to do with us as well.

Two major themes call for our attention as we examine this chapter. The first is the covenant which God established with Israel. The second is the mediation of this covenant.

The covenant God established with Israel

Are you confused about this matter of God establishing a covenant with the people of Israel? Did God not already have a covenant with these people?

The answer, of course, is that he did. Why, then, was this covenant necessary?

Let us review this matter of covenants. It is essential for us to understand that after Adam fell into sin, God announced his covenant of grace (Gen. 3:15). What is the covenant of grace? It is God pledging to restore sinners to friendship with himself through faith in the redeeming work of his Son, Jesus Christ. This covenant, planned before the world began and given in Eden, was later confirmed to Abraham (Gen. 12:1-3; 17:1-8; Gal. 3:16)

We must always keep in mind that the covenant of grace is the main covenant in the Bible. It is the controlling covenant.

The temptation when we come to the covenant of Exodus 19-24 is to think that God was setting aside the covenant of grace and doing something new. But that is not the case. The apostle Paul makes this abundantly plain when he says the law ' ... cannot annul the covenant that was confirmed before by God in Christ, ... ' (Gal. 3:17).

God did not give Israel the law, then, to replace or to nullify the covenant of grace. He rather gave it as a subsidiary covenant to further develop and manifest the covenant of grace.

How does the law God gave Israel do this? It was certainly not given so the people could earn their salvation by keeping the law. That would be the opposite of grace! It was rather given so the people of Israel could see their complete inability to keep the law. This would show the reality of their sin and cause them to look forward in faith to the Lord Jesus Christ who would do for them what they could not do for themselves.

The apostle Paul says: 'But the Scripture has confined all under sin, that the promise by faith in Jesus Christ might be given to those who believe' (Gal. 3:22).

With all this in place, we can consider three things about this covenant of law that God was going to establish with Israel.

The requirement

First, we have the requirement of the covenant. God puts it in these words: 'Now, therefore, if you will indeed obey My voice and keep My covenant' (v.5a).

God required them to obey this law. But, as we have already noted, they would most certainly find that they could not do so. The result would be the understanding that they needed the atonement for their sins that only the Messiah could provide.

The incentive

Then we have the incentive God gave them for keeping this covenant. He says: 'You have seen what I did to the Egyptians, and how I bore you on eagles' wings and brought you to Myself' (v.4).

As the mother eagle catches and carries her young when they are trying to fly, God had carried the Israelites out of slavery. How could the people not want to keep covenant with the God who had been so tremendously kind to them?

The promise

Finally, we have the promise of the covenant. God says: ' ... you shall be a special treasure to Me above all people; for all the earth is Mine. And you shall be to Me a kingdom of priests and a holy nation' (vv.5b-6a).

God had not chosen the Israelites because of any good thing in them (Deut. 7:7-8). It was entirely a matter of his grace. And it was for the purpose of having a people to spread his truth and to bring glory to his name. It is, by the way, the same with God's people of every generation. The apostle Peter says: 'But you are a chosen generation, a holy nation, His own special people, that you may proclaim the praises of Him who called you out of darkness into His marvelous light' (1 Peter 2:9-10).

The apostle Paul adds: 'Blessed by the God and Father of our Lord Jesus Christ, who has blessed us with every spiritual blessing in the heavenly places in Christ, just as He chose us in Him before the foundation of the world, that we should be holy and without blame before Him in love, having predestined us to adoption as sons by Jesus Christ to Himself, according to the good pleasure of His will, to the praise of the glory of His grace, by which He has made us accepted in the Beloved' (Eph. 1:3-6).

These Scriptures reveal that each and every child of God has been chosen by God every bit as much as the believing Israelites of old. Election means that God chose from the mass of sinful human beings people to be his own through the redeeming work of the Lord Jesus Christ. Because of the debilitating effects of sin, no one can come to God on his own. The fact that any sinner comes to God indicates that God has chosen him and applied the saving work of Christ to him. The doctrine of election unnerves and troubles many people. But the truth is that there could be no salvation apart from it.

That brings us to consider a second matter, that is...

The mediation of this covenant

It is impossible to read Exodus 19 without seeing the emphasis given to Moses (vv.3,6,7,8,9,10,14,15,17,19,20,21,23,24,25).

In these verses we find both the Lord speaking to Moses and Moses speaking to the people. It is very clear that Moses was to fill the role of a mediator.

Why was this necessary? Why did God not deal directly with the people themselves? Why did he put Moses in this role as a mediator between himself, God, and the people?

God is holy and people are sinful, and the only way sinful people can approach the holy God is through the mediator that God himself has approved.

The holiness of God is apparent in this chapter. The mountain was covered in smoke and 'quaked greatly' (v.18). Bounds were set so the people could not come near it or touch it (vv.12-13,23-24).

What does this have to do with us? We are dealing with the same God today!

Most people are so casual and careless about the things of God. As far as they are concerned, there is nothing to be feared from God. To their way of thinking, God loves everybody, and it is practically impossible to miss out on heaven. When such people encounter someone who takes the things of God very seriously, they wonder what all the fuss is about.

There is only one thing to say about such people. They have no idea with whom they are dealing! The holy God of the Old Testament is still alive and still holy, and the gap between him and guilty sinners is immeasurably wide!

No one can ever stand in the presence of this holy God and be accepted into his heaven until his sin has been taken out of the way.

How can sin be removed? We cannot remove it ourselves. But there is one who has come between the holy God and guilty sinners. He has bridged the gap between the two. He has come in the capacity of a mediator to reconcile the two.

Who is this? Let the apostle Paul answer: 'For there is one God one Mediator between God and men, the Man Christ Jesus, ...' (1 Tim. 2:5).

What has Jesus done in his capacity of mediator between God and sinners? Just as Moses declared the words of God to the people of Israel, so Jesus came as a prophet to proclaim the holiness of God, the sinfulness of men, the certainty of judgement and the way of salvation that he himself would provide. Moses himself would promise that the Messiah would come in this capacity of prophet (Deut. 18:18).

The Lord Jesus Christ also came as a priest. In that capacity he sacrificed himself for sinners. He was both the sacrificing priest and the sacrifice itself. Before God can have fellowship with sinners, the penalty for their sins must be paid. That penalty is the eternal wrath of God. Sinners must either pay it themselves or someone must pay it for them.

The Lord Jesus Christ could pay for the sins of others because he had no sins of his own for which to pay. On the cross he did pay for the sins of others. There he received an eternity's worth of wrath in the place of his people.

By receiving that penalty for them, the Lord Jesus took sin out of the way. It is no longer an impediment or barrier between the sinner and God, and the holy God can now have fellowship with the sinner who casts himself completely upon the atoning work of Jesus.

The one who believes in Christ need not live in dread of God. The terrors of the God of Mt. Sinai have yielded to the redeeming work of Jesus, who is 'the Mediator of the new covenant' (Heb. 12:24).

> *The terrors of law and of God*
> *With me can have nothing to do;*
> *My Saviour's obedience and blood*
> *Hide all my transgressions from view.*

> – Augustus Toplady

Old truths forgotten are truths just the same. The chapter before us contains forgotten truths, but the fact that we have forgotten them does not mean they are not true. Their truth will be fully revealed in due time as will the folly of all those who disregard them.

19 | The Ten Commandments

Exodus 20:1-17

God gave the people of Israel civil laws to regulate their relationships with one another and ceremonial laws to regulate and govern their worship. But the centrepiece of his covenant with them is the moral law which consists of the Ten Commandments.

What confusion swirls around these commandments! We should not be surprised that this is the case among people in general, but, sadly enough, it is also the case among Christians. I hope that some of this confusion will melt away as we consider three truths about these commandments.

First, we must note the God who gave the commandments (v.1)

The chapter opens with these words: 'And God spoke all these words'. Because this is the case, these commandments have both:

+ universal relevance – they are for everybody.
+ eternal relevance – they are for every era.

The Ten Commandments are at the very core of the cultural war that is going on in the United States. Those on one side of this cultural conflict are devoted to neutralizing, if not completely removing, the influence of Christianity from American society. One of their primary areas of attack is the Ten Commandments.

These people argue that the Ten Commandments were given in an ancient time to an ancient nation, and they have, therefore, no meaning or application for our time. A few years ago a media mogul made headlines by arguing that the Ten Commandments were out-moded and by proceeding to offer a set of his own!

This line of reasoning fails to give due weight to the God-given nature of these commandments. I hear someone saying: 'But that is the problem. I don't believe in the God of the Bible, and, therefore, I am not under his laws.'

But God's existence doesn't depend on human belief. He exists whether we believe in him or refuse to believe. He made this universe. We are his creatures. We breathe his air. We are all under his laws. And we will all finally be judged by him.

When Judgement Day rolls around, I suppose some people expect to tell God that they don't believe in him and – poof! – he will just disappear!

The God who gave these commandments to Israel is the God of all that is, and these commandments do not reflect his will for Israel alone but for all people. These commandments are the expression of his own moral character which never changes.

With that in place we can turn to consider...

The commandments which God gave (vv.2-17)

We find later that God wrote these commandments on two tables of stone (Exod. 32:15-16). By the way, the fact that they were etched in stone was undoubtedly meant to convey the permanence of these commandments. They were not given for only that period of time.

It is obvious that the commandments fall into two categories: those that pertain to our relationship to God and those that pertain to our relationship to other people.

There has been much debate about the proper division of the commandments. Some favour an unequal division. They insist that the Fifth Commandment (v.12), obedience to parents, has to do with our relationship to other people and must, therefore, belong to the second tablet.

Others favour an equal division. They place the Fifth Commandment with the first tablet and maintain that parents are God's representatives and invested with his authority. Honouring parents is to be considered, therefore, as part of our relationship to him.

Perhaps it is nothing more than my liking for tidiness that compels me to adopt the equal division. This, by the way, is the division that the Jews of old accepted.

The first table: duties to God

What, then, are our duties to God? We are to:

Place no other gods before him (v.3). We must have one God (there is no room for atheism), but we must have only one (there is no room for idolatry). In reality, there are no other gods but rather only those things which we make into gods. Nothing is to be given priority when doing so causes us to give the things of God a lesser place.

We are all by nature idolaters. We come into this world with a nature that is alienated from God and opposed to him. This nature constrains us to constantly elevate other things to that place that God alone should hold. The apostle Paul writes: 'There is none who seeks after God' (Rom. 3:11).

Left to ourselves, we are powerless to straighten the idolatrous bent of our hearts. We must have the regenerating work of the Holy Spirit to incline us toward God.

Make no image of God (vv.4-6). While the first commandment forbids allegiance to other gods, this commandment forbids worshipping the true God in the wrong way. It prohibits any kind of representation of God. The people of Israel saw no form of God, but only heard his Word. (Deut.4:12,15). They were, therefore, to make no image but rather obey God's Word.

This commandment shows us even more of our hearts, and it is not a pretty sight! We naturally go after idols, and we naturally distort the truth about the real God. We build in our minds a God that is not the God of the Bible. This is one with whom we can easily deal. He does not take sin seriously, does not threaten judgement and does not point unrelentingly to the redeeming death of his Son as the only way of salvation. He is rather an affable father who smiles indulgently at our sins and opens wide the door of heaven to us while we are still in our sins.

It is not unusual to hear someone preface a remark with these words: 'I prefer to think of God ... .' Those who do so are openly confessing their violation of the Second Commandment. They have constructed a mental image of God.

This commandment again shuts us up unto the knowledge of the Lord Jesus Christ. He and he alone gives the knowledge of the true God and inclines us to love that knowledge (John 1:14,18)

Refuse to treat God's name lightly (v.7). We are not to 'hollow' it, that is, empty it of its significance, but rather 'hallow' it, that is, always speaking to God and about him with reverence.

The way we speak about God reveals our attitude toward him. If we consistently speak of God in an irreverent and casual manner, it indicates that we do not hold him in awe and take him seriously. If this is our pattern, it shows that our hearts are in the grip of sin. The Lord Jesus said: 'How can you, being evil, speak good things? For out of the abundance of the heart the mouth speaks' (Matt. 12:34).

The more we see of our hearts, the more we realize that they need the touch of the regenerating grace of God.

Remember the Sabbath (vv.8-11). We are not to hijack God's day by treating it as if it were our own but rather use it to do those things that please him and further his kingdom.

'I don't have time,' are the words we often speak to excuse ourselves for not giving priority to God. But it is God who gives us time! To say we do not have time, then, is to say that we do not regard God highly enough to give him the portion of time he demands from all the time he gives us!

The trouble is not our busy-ness. It is once again our hearts.

Treat parents with honour and respect, recognizing their God-given authority (v.12). We are to be responsive to their commands in our younger years, sensitive to their needs in our older years and respectful through all the years.

The rejection of parental authority is tantamount to the rejection of God's authority from which the former is derived. Such rejection springs from a heart that despises authority. This commandment shows us that we are sinners. What is it to be a sinner? A.W. Pink answers: 'Sin is saying,

I renounce the God who made me; I disallow His right to govern me. I care not what He says to me, what commandments He has given, nor how He expostulates: I prefer self-indulgence to His approval. I am indifferent unto all He has done to and for me; His blessings and gifts move me not: I am going to be lord of myself.'[1]

The good news is that God gives sinners minds and hearts that freely acknowledge his authority and gladly submit to it.

The second table: duties to others

And what are our duties to others? We are not to:

Murder (v.13). We are to recognize that God is the creator of life and that the taking of it constitutes usurping his authority. It is impossible to honour God and refuse to honour our fellow-man who was made in his image.

We do not, as Jesus showed, keep this commandment by only refraining from murderous actions but also by refraining from hateful and murderous attitudes (Matt. 5:21-22). We cannot congratulate ourselves on keeping this commandment, then, only if we refrain from the external act. We are all murderers at heart and in need of the cleansing work of Christ.

Commit adultery (v.14). God has placed the good gift of sex within the context of marriage. All sexual behaviour outside that context is forbidden as is lustful desire (Matt. 5:27-30). We are all without exception indicted by this commandment as we are by the previous ones. If our sins are not forgiven, we face an eternity of separation from God. But, thank God, there is forgiveness through the Lord Jesus Christ who endured the penalty of the broken law in the place of all his people.

Steal (v.15). We are to respect those things which belong to others and refuse to treat them as if they were our own.

This commandment, like the others, is more far-reaching than most realize. We steal from God when we fail to obey the commandments of the first table. We steal from our fellow-man when we break the commandments of the second table. We even steal from ourselves by depriving ourselves of God's blessing through the breaking of his commandments. Is there any hope for thieves like us? Yes! Jesus Christ saves thieves! (Luke 23:39-43).

Lie (v.16). We are required to reject all forms of false, misleading and deceitful speech and to always speak truthfully and honestly.

Nothing is so indicative of the nature of our hearts and our condition before God than the way we talk. The tongue is the shop and the heart is the warehouse.

If we are to speak as God commands, we must have our hearts changed by God. Even then sin will continue to rear its head to the extent that we will have to cry with David:

> Set a guard, O Lord, over my
> mouth;
> Keep watch over the door of
> my lips (Ps. 141:3)

Covet (v.17). It is not sufficient for us to resist the overt actions that deprive others of those things which belong to them. We must not desire anything that belongs to another. This commandment shows that we are to treat all that belongs to our neighbour with respect. But it goes farther than that. Coveting is not a visible act. It is something that takes place within. This commandment makes explicit, then, what has been implicit all along, namely, that we are to comply with the laws of God with our hearts. Once again we must say that failure to do so gives us insight into the true nature of our hearts and our desperate need for the saving work of Christ.

The Lord Jesus summed up all of these commandments in these words: "You shall love the Lord your God with all your heart, with all your soul, and with all your mind.' This is the first and great commandment. And the second is like it: "You shall love your neighbor as yourself." On these commandments hang all the Law and the Prophets' (Matt. 22:37-40).

An example of the commandments at work

The apostle Paul serves as a powerful example of the point that we have been noticing all along, namely, the Ten Commandments were designed to make us conscious of our sinfulness and to drive us to Christ (Rom. 7:7-12; Phil. 3:1-11).

Paul knew something that most people seem not to know, namely, that God requires perfect righteousness to enter heaven. No one will ever enter there who has not perfectly conformed to the laws of God.

For a long time, Paul thought he was doing very well. He could go down the list of these Ten Commandments and check them off one by one, saying with each checkmark: 'I've kept that one.'

Paul continued to do well until it dawned on him that the Ten Commandments require internal compliance as well as outward. In particular, Paul came to see that he had failed to keep the final commandment which prohibits coveting (Rom. 7:7-11). While his outward conduct was above reproach, he had broken the commandments of God internally by having sinful thoughts and desires.

Paul was crushed with despair. Here God was demanding perfect righteousness, and here he, Paul, was far short of that righteousness. What could he do? Where could he turn?

The situation would seem to have been hopeless, but it was not. Paul came to see that while he himself did not have the righteousness that God demanded, there was one who did – the Lord Jesus Christ. While he, Paul, had violated the law of God, Jesus never did.

Paul further came to see that the righteousness of Jesus could count for him if he would abandon all hopes of producing righteousness himself and depend completely on Christ (Phil. 3:8-9).

So the Ten Commandments had achieved their purpose in Paul. They had caused him to see the reality and enormity of his sin and had driven him to faith in the Lord Jesus Christ.

God gave these commandments, not so we could earn salvation by keeping them, but rather so we could see how sinful we are, how incapable we are of keeping them and how desperately we need the saving work of the Lord Jesus Christ. The apostle Paul says: ' ... the law was our tutor to bring us to Christ, that we might be justified by faith' (Gal. 3:24).

While we cannot be saved by keeping the Ten Commandments, we must remember that they remain as an accurate reflection of what pleases God. The Christian must, therefore, seek to keep them as an expression of gratitude to the God who has saved us.

One commentator says of Israel: 'The Law could never bring people to salvation, because none of us is capable of keeping it all. Rather, now that the people were freed and saved they needed to order their lives to fit in with the expressed will of God.'[2]

That statement applies equally to every Christian today.

20 | The Tabernacle and the Ark of the Covenant

Exodus 25:10-22; 26:31-35

God had more to give Moses on Mt. Sinai than the Ten Commandments. While he was there, God also gave him instructions for building the Tabernacle and for making the furnishings which were to be placed in it (26:30).

It cannot be said often enough or strongly enough that the Tabernacle and all its furnishings were designed to point to the Lord Jesus Christ. The Bible knows only one way of salvation, and that way is the redeeming work of Christ.

I want us to consider how the Tabernacle and the ark of the covenant point us to Christ. All the furnishings of the Tabernacle have some connection with Christ, but all are agreed that the ark of the covenant is the main piece in the Tabernacle.

Before we delve into these matters, it is essential for us to notice the precision of the instructions God gave for building and supplying the Tabernacle. These things all had to do with his redeeming work, and God was very, very precise. He didn't tell Moses to build the Tabernacle any way he, Moses, wanted. He didn't tell him to put the various furnishings wherever he wanted. No, not at all! God was very specific about each detail.

Sinful men and women do not share God's precision on salvation. While they embrace precision in other areas of life, they resent and resist it on the matter of eternal salvation. To most people salvation is a matter of believing what they want. Everyone has his own view, and who is to say which view is correct!

The Tabernacle and the ark are against such views. They speak forcefully about the situation which requires salvation and the only way that situation can be resolved.

The Tabernacle

The Tabernacle was designed to convey both God's presence and his distance.

It conveyed his presence in that it was there among the Israelites. They could see it.

But the fact that the Tabernacle indicated the presence of God did not mean the Israelites could establish a chummy familiarity with him.

The Tabernacle consisted of three major divisions. First, there was the outer court. This was the area into which the people could come. Then there was the holy place. This was the area in which the priests carried out their responsibilities. Finally, there was the Most Holy Place (26:33-34). This was the place into which only the high priest of Israel could enter. But he could not enter at any time that he wanted. He could not slip into the Most Holy Place for a little quiet time or for a coffee break. He could enter only once a year, on the Day of Atonement, and when he entered he had to have with him the blood of a sacrificed animal.

It is also significant that the Most Holy Place was sealed off from the holy place with a heavy, thick veil (26:31-33).

All of this cries 'Distance! Distance!' Why was there such distance between God and the people. God is holy and people are sinful! Sinful people cannot just waltz into the presence of God and enjoy his fellowship without atonement being made for their sins.

Is there an atonement for sinners? There is in the death of the Lord Jesus Christ on the cross. When he died, the veil in the temple was ripped from top to bottom (Matt. 27:50-51). Jesus bridged the distance between the holy God and sinful people! How did he do this? We can find the answer by looking at...

The ark of the covenant

Because of the popular movie Raiders of the Lost Ark, most people now know about this item. It was a box overlaid with gold with a slab of solid gold above it and cherubim on each side with their wings outstretched over the box.

Inside the box were the tables of stone on which God had written the Ten Commandments. This represented God's holy character and God's demand for his people to be holy. These commandments describe for us the holiness that God demands. Scripture clearly shows that holiness is not just a matter of obeying these commandments in an external sort of way. God requires holiness in our desires as well as in our actions (Ps. 51:6; Matt. 22:37; Rom. 7:7,22).

In addition to these things, the Lord prescribed eternal death for those who failed to keep his commandments.

As the Israelites of old reflected upon God's demands, they were filled with despair. What hope was there for people who had broken God's laws and stood under his sentence of eternal wrath? The ark of God gave the answer to that piercing question.

It is interesting that the mercy seat on top of the ark was exactly the same width as the box containing the law. That mercy seat was the place where the blood of atonement was sprinkled by the high priest on the annual Day of Atonement. This indicated that the blood of atonement perfectly satisfied the demands of God's law.

It is also striking that the cherubim were looking down at the mercy seat. The cherubim are the highest of the angels. Because they are associated with the throne of God in Scripture, we can understand them to represent God himself.

The fact that the cherubim on the ark looked down at the mercy seat where the blood was sprinkled by the priest takes us to the heart of the meaning of the atonement. The cherubim, representing God, did not see the law and its demands because it was inside the box which was covered by the mercy seat where the blood fell.

When the high priest of Israel went into the Most Holy Place and sprinkled the blood of the sacrifice on the mercy seat, it indicated that the demand of God's law for the death of the sinner had been satisfied. The blood of the mercy seat covered the demand of the law. A.W. Pink writes: 'Suppose an Ark with no Mercy-seat: the Law would then be uncovered: there would be nothing to hush its thunderings, nothing to arrest the execution of its righteous sentence.'[1]

Thank God for the Mercy-seat!

Those who think that the Old Testament is the account of God vainly searching for a plan of salvation would do well to look at the ark of God.

It was a glorious anticipation of the death of the Lord Jesus Christ on the cross. The apostle Paul says God the Father 'set forth' Christ as a 'propitiation' (Rom. 3:25). The Greek word translated 'propitiation' in this verse is translated as 'mercy seat' in Hebrews 9:5. By his death on the cross, the Lord Jesus Christ became our mercy seat.

To propitiate means to appease or placate wrath or anger. We have a tendency to think of Christ's death on the cross in terms of what it provided for us, that is, forgiveness of our sins and right standing before God. How seldom is it understood that the cross was primarily intended to do something for God!

God's holy character is such that he is deeply insulted and offended by our sins. It is such that he is compelled to judge sin. He must carry out the sentence that he himself has pronounced upon the sinner, that is, eternal death. Only through the execution of that sentence can God's wrath against sin be placated or satisfied. If that sentence were not executed God would not be just.

There are only two ways for this sentence to be carried out. Either the sinner himself must bear the sentence or someone must bear it in his place. The good news of the gospel is that God placated his own wrath against his people by pouring it out on his Son as their substitute.

On the cross Jesus fulfilled that which the types of the Old Testament could only anticipate and portray. There Jesus was both the high priest who offered the sacrifice and the sacrifice itself. He offered himself to God as the sacrifice for sinners. Drawing on the imagery of the Old Testament, we can say that the Lord Jesus sprinkled his blood on the mercy seat of heaven (Heb. 9:1-28), and now believing sinners have nothing to fear from the law that demanded their condemnation. The blood of Christ fulfils that demand.

By his death on the cross Jesus completely and eternally satisfied both God's justice and mercy. Justice was satisfied because Jesus received upon the cross the full measure of God's wrath against sinners. And mercy was also satisfied because, since Jesus took God's wrath on behalf of the believing sinner, no wrath left for that sinner to endure. Justice only demands that the penalty of sin be paid once, and, if Jesus has paid it, nothing is left for the one who is in Jesus to pay.

Exodus 28:1-38

The clothing a high priest wore thousands of years ago may seem to have little or no meaning for us. Closer examination will show us that these articles of clothing portray truths that are of on-going validity for us. It is not too much to say that our personal well-being is bound up in these clothes.

Preliminary considerations

The God-ordained nature of the high priest's clothes

To understand Exodus 28, we must go to Exodus 25:1 and these words: 'Then the Lord spoke to Moses, saying.'

The words of Exodus 28 are the continuation of the Lord's words to Moses. Why is this important? It shows us that the clothing of the high priest was not something that Moses and Aaron arrived at on their own. It was not the product of the work of a 'Worship Committee.' It was the result of God speaking and laying out in detail what this clothing was to be like.

It is not too much to say that Christianity exists because God has spoken. The Christian faith is not something that men contrived. Christians hold certain truths because God has revealed them.

The purpose behind this clothing

The Lord tells Moses that Aaron was to minister to him, the Lord, as priest (vv.1,4).

It was the task of the high priest of Israel to represent his people before God by making sacrifices for their sins and by interceding on their behalf.

This work was of such vital and crucial importance that it had to be done in a certain way. Casual irreverence was completely unacceptable. It was necessary, therefore, for Aaron to be attired in 'holy garments … for glory and for beauty' (v.2).

With these things in place, we are ready to consider…

The articles of clothing

The ephod (vv.5-14)

The ephod was something of an apron that was woven with gold, blue, purple and scarlet threads. Particular emphasis is given to the two shoulder straps. Each strap had on it two onyx stones, each of which had the names of six of the tribes of Israel (vv.7-12). The purpose of this is made clear. When Aaron went into the Holy Place, it would be as the bearer of the burdens of his people.

If we considered no other article of the high priest's clothing, we would have reason to rejoice with 'joy unspeakable and full of glory.' This article points us to the Lord Jesus Christ who bears the burdens of his people.

The most oppressive of all these burdens is, of course, the burden of sin and condemnation. The Lord Jesus shouldered this burden on the cross. There he bore the full weight of it, receiving the wrath of God in the stead of his people.

But that act of burden-bearing did not end the functioning of Jesus in this role. He continues to bear the burdens of all his people.

The breastplate

Verses 15-30 call our attention to the breastplate of the high priest. This was a nine inch square 'pocket.' On the outside were four rows of precious stones with three stones in each row. Each stone bore one of the names of the twelve tribes of Israel.

The tribes' names on the shoulders indicated, as we have noted, the high priest bearing their burdens. Their names on the breastplate indicated that he also carried them on his heart.

This is also a portrayal of the Lord Jesus Christ. In addition to having the strength to bear our burdens, he cares deeply about us and the burdens we bear. The apostle Peter says we can cast our burdens on him because 'He cares for you' (1 Peter 5:7).

The Urim and Thummim (vv.30-31)

Inside the pocket were two stones, called the Urim and Thummim. One of these stones represented the curse, or the negative, the other represented the blessing, or the positive. These stones were to be used to discover the will of God especially in times of crisis.

The Urim and Thummim also point to Christ 'in whom are hidden all the treasures of wisdom and knowledge' (Col. 2:3).

The closer we live to Christ – walking in communion with him, obeying his commands, exalting him in worship, following his example, reading his Word, rendering service in his name – the less we will need to worry about finding his will. When we put ourselves in the proper place and devote our energies to the proper concern, the will of Christ will find us.

The blue robe

Verses 31-35 describe the blue robe, which was to be slipped over the head. Bells and golden pomegranates were to be hung in alternating fashion on its hem.

The pomegranate was a fruit that was particularly abundant in the promised land of Canaan. Use of it on the robe may have been merely 'for beauty' (v.2) or as a reminder to the people that God would most surely give them the land in which this fruit abounded.

While there is some uncertainty about the reason for the pomegranates being included on the robe, there is no doubt about the bells. The high priest alone was to enter into the Most Holy Place of the tabernacle once a year to make atonement for the sins of the people. This atonement had to be made in precisely the way the Lord commanded. If the high priest failed in any respect, he would die there in the Most Holy Place.

The jingling of the bells indicated to those outside that the high priest was performing his duties acceptably. If they stopped jingling, it meant he had failed and was dead. Since the high priest alone could enter the Most Holy Place, it has been assumed that a rope was attached to one of his ankles to pull him out if he died!

In these casual and irreverent days in which there is little regard for truth, we would do well to ponder this: God is very precise about this matter of eternal salvation for sinners.

Many seem to assume that it is almost impossible to miss out on heaven. But God makes it plain that sinners can only enter his presence if atonement has been made for their sins – an atonement that is pleasing to him.

The Lord Jesus is, of course, the one who made that perfect atonement. On the cross, he, as we have noted, bore the wrath of God in the place of his people. His resurrection and ascension prove beyond any shadow of doubt that God was pleased with that atonement.

The turban or headpiece (vv.36-38)

This was to have on it a plate of gold with the words: HOLINESS TO THE LORD (v.36).

Michael Bentley explains this turban and gold plate in this way: 'When the high priest entered the Holy Place, symbolically bearing the guilt of the people, his mediation and sacrifices he offered on their behalf would make the gifts the people had consecrated acceptable to the Lord.'[1]

Matthew Henry applies this part of Aaron's work to Christ: 'Through him what is amiss in our services is pardoned. The divine law is strict; in many things we come short of our duty, so that we cannot but be conscious to ourselves of much iniquity cleaving even to our holy things; … But Christ, our high priest, bears this iniquity, bears it for us so as to bear it from us, and through him it is forgiven to us and not laid to our charge.'[2]

Henry makes a second application in these words: 'Through him what is good is accepted; our persons, our performances, are pleasing to God upon the account of Christ's intercession, and not otherwise.'[3]

The garments God appointed for Aaron and his successors are long gone. But the true High Priest to whom these garments pointed, the Lord Jesus Christ, lives on and ministers 'according to the power of an endless life' (Heb. 6:16). He is today the High Priest who has born and continues to bear the burdens of his people because he carries them on his heart. He is the High Priest who guides his people. He is the High Priest who makes the service of his people acceptable to God. And he is able to do all this on the basis of his totally sufficient atonement. How very thankful we should be for such a High Priest!

Exodus 32

The nation of Israel, under the leadership of Moses, had at this time been released from their bondage in Egypt only a very brief time (19:1). They were encamped at the foot of Mt. Sinai while Moses was meeting with the Lord on the mountain (24:12).

It is important for us to understand that Moses had already made one trip up the mountain to receive the Ten Commandments and other instructions. He had reported these to the people (19:3;25; 24:3) who very readily embraced them with this resounding affirmation: 'All the words which the Lord has said we will do' (24:3).

There was no ambiguity at all about the second of these commandments: 'You shall not make for yourself a carved image—any likeness of anything that is in heaven above, or that is in the earth beneath, or that is in the water under the earth; you shall not bow down to them nor serve them' (20:4-5a).

There was also no ambiguity about the terrible cost attached to disobeying this commandment. After stating it, the Lord had proceeded to add these words: 'For I, the Lord your God, am a jealous God, visiting the iniquity of the fathers upon the children to the third and fourth generations of those who hate Me, but showing mercy to thousands, to those who love Me and keep My commandments' (20:5b).

If those words did not provide enough incentive for the people of Israel to obey this commandment, all they had to do was review the recent expressions of God's goodness to them. He had delivered them from grinding, oppressive bondage in Egypt and had borne them to himself on 'eagles' wings' (19:4). Furthermore, he had promised to make them his own special treasure, a kingdom of priests and a holy nation (19:5-6).

Such kindness in the past coupled with such a promise for the future would appear to make obedience to God's commandments the delight of every Israelite heart. But the clarity of the commandment, the incentives to obey it and their own hearty endorsement of it were not sufficient for those hearts. Only forty days (24:18) after Moses again ascended the mountain, the people gathered around Aaron and began clamouring for him to lead the way in a flagrant rebellion against the second commandment.

The cause of their idolatry

What possessed them to do such a thing? They pleaded the absence of Moses (v.1). To them it was unthinkable that he could be gone so long and still return. This was a quite remarkable assumption in light of the fact that God had used Moses to announce their deliverance from Egypt (6:5-7) and to assure them that they would receive the land promised to their fathers (6:8). Moses was also the instrument God used to rain plagues down upon Pharaoh and all of Egypt (7:14-12:30). And he actually led the people out of Egypt and into the Sinaitic wilderness (12:31-39; 13:17-14:31).

All of this would seem to indicate that God was not about to set the man aside before the task of bringing the people into Canaan was complete. But the people of Israel were not interested in thinking deeply and seriously about God's dealings with them and about what those dealings suggested, that is, their God was entirely faithful.

The truth is the absence of Moses did not really matter that much to them. It just happened to be a handy pretext for them to put into practice what was in their hearts. And what was that? If we fast forward several centuries to the book of Acts, we find the godly Stephen giving an inspired account of the golden calf episode, and he has nothing at all to say about the absence of Moses. He did, however, offer this telling explanation: ' … in their hearts they turned back to Egypt' (Acts 7:39).

The absence of Moses was, then, nothing more than a convenient outer reality for them to yield to an inner reality: hearts that were still in Egypt.

Egypt was all these people knew, and, as Joshua was to plainly state, many of them had served the visible gods of Egypt (Josh. 24:14). Now they were away from Egypt and called upon to serve an invisible God, a God who so blazed in holiness, that they could not approach him without

Moses as their mediator. Perhaps it was the desire to have what Michael Horton calls 'a greasy familiarity'[1] with God that caused them to yearn for gods such as they had worshipped in Egypt. As far as they were concerned, Moses' absence gave them the perfect opportunity to satisfy that yearning. So they put the proposition to Aaron (v.1), the golden calf was made (vv.2-4) and a celebration was held (vv.5-6) which had more to do with sex than religion (the Hebrew word translated 'rose up to play' is also used in Genesis 26:8 where it definitely has sexual overtones).

The deficiency of their idolatry

Were these people thinking of this golden calf as a new god or only as a new and better way to worship the God who had brought them out of Egypt? Stephen's statement in the book of Acts indicates that they were thinking in terms of the gods they had worshipped in Egypt and were, therefore, embracing a new god. But it is noteworthy that Aaron proclaimed the day of celebration by using the covenant name for God (v.5). It is possible that some of the people thought of the calf in one way while others thought of it in another way.

Even if most of the people viewed this calf as a new and improved way of worshipping the true God, they were dreadfully mistaken. The calf or bull, a symbol of power, was obviously intended to honour the power of God. But any image of God does the exact opposite of what it is intended to do. It obscures rather than reveals God. The golden calf could not do justice to God's power which, unlike the calf's, is unlimited. And the image of the calf completely excluded all the other attributes of God. God is more than power. He is also omnipresent, omniscient, holy, just, wise, merciful, gracious, faithful and eternal. The calf was, therefore, actually derogatory to the very one it purported to honour because it minimalized and localized him.

Nothing is more sickening and pathetic in all of this than Aaron's role. Given the opportunity to stand for God and truth in this situation, he meekly complied with the desire of the people (vv.2-5), and, when called to account by Moses, lamely explained that he just threw the gold in the fire and the calf miraculously emerged (vv.21-24).

The results of their idolatry

It all came to a screeching halt with a crushing judgement of immense proportions (vv.25-28). After burning the calf and reducing it to powder, Moses sprinkled it in water and forced the people to drink it (v.20). All of this was designed to drive home the utter helplessness of their god. A god that cannot keep itself from being burned and ground up is not much of a god. A god that can be imbibed by its devotees is even less than they. Imagine having a god that can be worshipped one moment and drank the next!

Naked Israelites dancing feverishly around a golden calf! It all sounds very crude and far removed from us, but it isn't. Calves are still popping out of the fire. When we give to anything the allegiance and devotion that belong to God alone, we are guilty of idolatry. If we put money before God, we have an idol. If we put pleasure before God, we have an idol. It is the same with our careers and even our families.

Idolatry can be even more subtle. When we make the God of the Bible to conform to our own liking, we have an idol.

There is not a hair-breadth's change in the true God since that ancient day. He is still the God who flames with glory and holiness, and, just as Israel of old could not approach him except through the mediatorial work of Moses, so we can know him only through the true Mediator whom Moses was intended to foreshadow. That Mediator is none other than the Lord Jesus Christ (1 Tim. 2:5).

But many do not want this kind of God. They prefer one who is user-friendly and seeker-sensitive. As the Israelites thought of themselves as being sovereign in the area of worship, so it is easy for us to think of ourselves in the same way. We pride ourselves on knowing what is best and what 'sells.' And a majestic, glorious God who is clothed in mystery and condemns sin is not what sells. A God who insists that there is only one way of salvation, and that way is the redeeming work of his Son on a bloody Roman cross doesn't sell. What sells is a God who is tame and non-threatening, one who is not concerned about us serving him but with serving us. What sells is a God who busies himself with helping us manage the problems and circumstances of our lives. We are not concerned with God getting us safely into eternity but only with him getting us comfortably through another week. And preachers and churches, who, shades of Aaron, are ever anxious to please, are dumbing down and de-glorifying

God in order to give people what they want. Worship services are light and cheery. Reverence is considered to be out-dated and laughable. Holiness, faithfulness, commitment, responsibility and discipline are obscene words. Sin, guilt, condemnation and a blood atonement are muted.

Even though there is much in the modern day church to lament, there is still consolation and hope. There is a Mediator, the Lord Jesus Christ. He is still at the right hand of God to make intercession for his people, to bring them to repent of their idolatry and to grant forgiveness when they do (1 John 2:1).

23 | The Tent of Meeting

Exodus 33:7-11

We now have before us a powerful and moving passage of Scripture. Here Moses sets up the tent of meeting outside the camp of Israel. We must not confuse this tent with the tabernacle, which had not yet been constructed (Exod. 35-40).

Let's get our bearings. The Israelites were still encamped at the foot of Mt. Sinai. There God gave them his laws, who, after heartily subscribing to them, plunged into idolatry of the most shocking sort.

Although Moses had dealt very sternly with the idolatry, its cloud was still hanging heavy over Israel. The passage we are about to consider is tied to that idolatry. Moses set up the tent of meeting for the purpose of seeking genuine spiritual renewal. It was not enough for the people to turn away from their idols. They must also wholeheartedly turn back to God.

If this tent of meeting had to do with spiritual renewal or revival, it is just as important for us as it was for Moses' people. We need revival as much as they. While we have not made calves of gold to worship, we definitely have our idols. And those idols have displeased the Lord and have driven a wedge between him and us.

This tent of meeting enables us to answer some vital questions about the issue of revival.

When is revival necessary?

The answer is already before us, that is, when we, the people of God, have displeased him.

How displeased God was with the Israelites! Notice that he first refers to them as Moses' people, saying to Moses: 'Depart and go up from here, you and the people whom you have brought out of the land of Egypt' (v.1).

Notice, secondly, that he only promises to send his angel to go with them (vv.2-3). God is so displeased that he says they can go on without him!

Consider in the third place the description he places on them. He calls them 'a stiff-necked people' (v.3). They would not bow their heads in submission to him. They were obstinate, stubborn and rebellious.

In addition to these things, Moses set the tent of meeting up 'outside the camp' (v.7), as if to indicate the distance between them and God and God's desire not to be close to them.

We would do well to ponder these things. We have the notion that God is so choked up with love for his people that he lightly dismisses their sins. This episode tells us that God's people can sorely displease him, and that it is a serious thing when they do. This is precisely what many churches and individual Christians have done. They have deeply grieved God and driven him away. They have done so by:

+ refusing to stand for the truth of his Word but eagerly bartering it away in order to accommodate the thinking and doing of this age.

+ going through worship services as religious consumers who are more concerned about being entertained than they are about worshipping God in spirit and in truth.

+ refusing to keep God's commandments by both failing to do those things he requires and by doing those things he forbids.

+ dropping our responsibilities to him in order to chase after pleasures and material things.

The list could go on and on. And at the end of it, we are confronted with this stark reality: that which the modern day church calls 'worship' is often directed to an absent God and what she calls 'service' is often for a withdrawn God. And the same goes for individual believers.

Nothing is more wonderful than the presence of God, and nothing is sadder and more tragic than the absence of God.

But what is the remedy for such a sorrowful state of affairs? In other words...

When does revival come?

The tent of meeting Moses provides the answer. It tells us that God's people can expect revival when they so feel the burden of the times that they are willing to take special measures to seek God's face.

Our passage shows that there was an encouraging sign along these lines before Moses set up the tent. Verse 4 says: 'And when the people heard these grave tidings, they mourned, and no one put on his ornaments.'

These people, realizing the gravity of their situation, were unwilling to go about their lives as usual. They felt such inward grief over the loss of God's presence that they expressed it outwardly.

In doing so, they put themselves far ahead of today's church. How few grieve over the loss of God's presence! As long as the church machinery keeps running – churning out more and more programs and producing good numbers – church leaders are willing to overlook the absence of any real spiritual power. And as long as their lives are comfortable, individual Christians are willing to do the same.

A 'business as usual' attitude will never bring revival. Many of the people of Israel understood this. Do we?

Moses understood this so well that he set up the tent of meeting. This tent provided a place for the people of Israel to go to seek the Lord. Verse 7 concludes with these words: 'And it came to pass that everyone who sought the Lord went out to the tabernacle of meeting which was outside the camp.'

Martyn Lloyd-Jones writes: 'generally the very first thing that happens, and which eventually leads to a great revival is that one man, or a group of men, suddenly begin to feel this burden, and they feel the burden so much that they are led to do something about it.'[1]

If we want to see true revival, we must take special measures. We must set aside time to seek God. We must gather with other Christians. We must go 'outside the camp.' That means we must lay aside the regular activities of life to seek the Lord. Imagine that! Laying aside the things of life to seek the very one who gives them to us!

While Bible-believing churches these day do not set up tents of meeting per se, they offer an equivalent any time they call a meeting for the express purpose of seeking the Lord. Such meetings give the people of God a time and place to seek God, to ask him to come back among his people in power to bless them. How few are interested in such! When they come around, many are unwilling to lay anything aside. They are unwilling to go 'outside the camp'. They are content to do as many in Moses' day did, that is, stand by and look on (v.8). They would rather have the church muddle and fumble along without the presence and power of God than to do what is necessary to have that power.

Why is there such little interest in such meetings? Why is there such little interest in seeking God? The sad answer has to be that most church members do not realize that he is missing! Meanwhile we have family members, friends and neighbours who are marching steadily to eternal woe.

It takes the power of God to convert sinners, and that power is largely being withheld because the church has grieved the Lord with her apathy and her idolatry.

What happens when revival comes?

Moses' tent of meeting achieved its purpose. This passage tells us that the pillar of cloud, which symbolized God's presence, 'stood at the door of the tabernacle' (v.9).

That cloud, symbolizing God's presence, had been withdrawn while the people were occupied with their calf. But now, as a result of Moses and many of the people seeking God, it comes back.

If we will seek the Lord, we can rest assured that he will be found. We can be confident of this because of the promise he has given:' … if My people who are called by My name will humble themselves, and pray and seek My face, and turn from their wicked ways, then I will hear from heaven, and will forgive their sin and heal their land' (2 Chron. 7:14).

24 | Moses in prayer

Exodus 33:12-23

What would you say is the main thing going on in this world? Political strategies are being set. Sporting events are going on. Seminars on the various moral and ethical issues are being offered. Scientific research is being conducted. But none of these qualify as the most important activity. That place must be awarded to prayer.

While some activities - such as the preaching and teaching of the gospel – are as important as prayer, nothing is more important. Little do we realize the importance of prayer. If we did, we would devote ourselves more fully to it. When the eternal day dawns, we will finally realize its value, and we will be ashamed that we were so little occupied with it. We will then understand these words from Henry Law: 'Earth owes much to supplicating lips.'[1]

We should always be interested in any passage of Scripture that sets prayer before us. We should be especially interested in those portions that set before us the best and most heroic of people engaging in prayer. Our text is one such passage. Here Moses, one of the best of men, is engaged in this most important activity of prayer.

We noted in our last study how Moses set up the tent of meeting for the express purpose of seeking the Lord. This was necessary because of the egregious sin of the Israelites in worshipping the golden calf.

This passage makes it clear that Moses did not merely erect this tent. He made use of it. Here we have an account of some petitions he offered to the Lord.

Moses prays to know God's way (vv.12-13)

The way of the Lord must have appeared at this time to be utterly mysterious to Moses. God had said that he would not go with the people to the land of Canaan (v.3) but would send his angel (v.2). To this point, however, he had not identified the angel (v.12). Moses must have wondered how it was possible for Israel to be God's people while God himself refused to be present with them. And if they were not God's people, how could God's covenant with them be fulfilled? He also may have wondered how God could send his angel to lead the people and not be present himself.

Moses was a man with a dilemma, but he was also a man with a resource. He went to the Lord in prayer, speaking very candidly to God about his confusion and bewilderment.

The ways of God often seem very strange and bewildering to us. Why do God's people suffer? Why do the wicked prosper? Why does God not advance his work more quickly and give more evidences of himself? With these and a hundred other questions begging to be answered, what are we to do? We are to pray. We are to tell the Lord all about it. We are to ask him to more fully reveal himself to us, to give us more intimate knowledge of himself and to enable us to trust him even when his ways are perplexing.

Such praying may not answer all the questions, but it will bring strength into our lives that will enable us to go forward with peace. It will make us understand that the Christian does not believe because he has the answers to all questions, but rather because he has enough answers to enough questions that he cannot help but believe. And it will give us the persuasion that the rest of the answers will come in glory.

Moses prays to have God's presence (vv.14-17)

The Lord responded to Moses' first petition with these words: 'My presence will go with you, and I will give you rest' (v.14).

The Lord was referring to Moses alone. He was essentially saying: 'Moses, my withdrawal from my people does not mean I have withdrawn from you. I will be with you even though I will not be with them. And my presence with you will be sufficient for you.'

But Moses would not settle for this. He says: 'If Your Presence does not go with us, do not bring us up from here' (v.15).

Here we have Moses functioning again as the mediator between God and the people. While God says 'you,' Moses says 'us.' He would not have for himself that which his people could not share.

We surely cannot read this without finding ourselves driven to the Lord Jesus Christ as the Mediator for his people. Alexander Maclaren says of him: 'He, too, knits Himself so closely with us, both by the assumption of our manhood and by the identity of loving sympathy, that He accepts nothing from the Father's hand for Himself alone. He, too, presents Himself before God, and says "I and Thy people."'[2]

This situation has far more to do with us than most of us realize. It is not just a piece of meaningless antiquity. The church of today and individual Christians can be found in every line of this portion of Exodus. As the Israelites grieved God and drove him away with their idolatry, so have we. But how few seem to feel the absence of God these days! The church machinery grinds on, and we claim God's blessing. But peel back the veneer of success, and there is little evidence of God being powerfully present among his people. How much is there about God's people that makes it clear that they are separate from 'all the people who upon the face of the earth'? (v.16).

Of this we may be sure – God only returns in power to his people when they feel the loss of his presence, grieve over it and persistently say to him: 'We must have your presence. Nothing we do will matter if you are not present!'

What a wonderful answer Moses received for this petition! The Lord said: 'I will also do this thing that you have spoken; … ' (v.17). But we must notice God's reason for returning to his people: ' … for you have found grace in My sight, and I know you by name' (v.17b).

It was for Moses' sake that the Lord agreed to return to his people. Let this remind us that every blessing we receive from God is not because we are worthy or deserving. It is rather because of our connection with the Lord Jesus Christ who is our Mediator.

Moses prays to see God's glory (vv.18-23)

It would seem to have been the appropriate time for Moses to end his prayer. The most critical issue had now been resolved. God had agreed to be present again with the people. But Moses could not be content to leave matters there. He adds yet another request: 'Please, show me Your glory' (v.18).

This is what Alexander Maclaren calls Moses' 'last soaring desire.'[3]

Do you and I know what it is to have a 'soaring desire'? Do we know what it is to fervently long for something of an extraordinary nature? Maclaren rightly says: 'Our desires keep but too well within the limits of the possible.'[4]

What extraordinary things Moses had seen from God! But he desires more. He asks for the whole package. He wants to see all the glory of God. He wants to know God fully.

He did not understand that for which he was asking. God was far more glorious than he realized, so much so that no one can see him and live to tell the story (v.20). What a God!

The God of such glory is also a God of grace. While he could not show Moses all his glory, he could and would pass by while Moses stood in the cleft of a rock. While shielded there, Moses would be enabled to see his back (v.23).

Don't feel sorry for Moses. He did not get cheated. God is so glorious that a mere glimpse of his back took Moses to a higher level than he had ever been before.

It is hard not to see in Moses' experience yet another exciting picture of the gospel of Christ. We have already established in this series that the rock symbolizes the Lord Jesus. On Calvary's cross, he was 'cleft', that is, opened or split. As you and I hide in the crucified Christ, we are able to see something of the glory of God's wisdom and grace – wisdom that found a way to redeem us and grace that desired to redeem us. And there we can take as our own the words of Augustus M. Toplady:

> Rock of ages, cleft for me,
> Let me hide myself in Thee.
> Let the water and the blood,
> From Thy wounded side which flowed,

> *Be of sin the double cure,*
> *Save from wrath and make me pure.*

I cannot help but think that we also find in Moses' experience something of the nature of true revival. It is God's people getting a glimpse of his glory. How urgently we should be praying for this!

We have gone with Moses, then, into the prayer closet. We may rest assured that we will never be able to pray as this man of God prayed. But we can pray! Let us be doing so. Let us heed the words of Henry Law: 'Believer, in every place, and at every time drop seeds of prayer. The crop may live when your short race is run.'[5]

Exodus 34:1-9

In the Tent of Meeting, Moses asked to see God's glory (33:18). The Lord responded by saying that it was impossible for any man to see his face (33:20). But the Lord also promised that he would pass before Moses and proclaim his name and his goodness to him (33:19).

These verses deal with the fulfilment of that promise. Moses did not receive the fulfilment immediately after he prayed there in the Tent of Meeting. He had to wait until the next morning on Mt. Sinai.

Then and there Moses received a glimpse of the glory of God. As God passed by, he stood in the cleft of a rock and saw the back of God, just as God promised (33:21-23). And Moses heard God proclaim his name and his goodness (34:5-7).

It is an unspeakable privilege to hear a man of God accurately proclaim the truth of God. What a privilege Moses enjoyed – the blessed privilege of hearing God proclaim himself!

Why should we be interested in this? The answer is not hard to find. We are dealing with the very same God as Moses, and what was true of God on this occasion is still true.

Let's eagerly examine, then, both the proclamation of God's name and the proclamation of his goodness.

The proclamation of God's name (vv.5-6a)

The names God uses are found in the phrase 'The Lord, the Lord God' (v.6).

In using the name 'Lord,' God was repeating the name by which he had revealed himself to Moses at the burning bush (Exod. 3:14).

The first thing God did in his revelation to Moses, therefore, was to remind him that he was the very same God who had originally revealed himself to him. He was still the self-existent, self-sufficient, eternal God. He had not changed one iota.

The fact that this name, 'the Lord,' is repeated should be taken as God emphasizing the point. God did not want Moses to underestimate or minimize the revelation that he had been given at the burning bush.

Henry Law writes: 'This repetition bids us look again. It tells us that thought upon thought must search the mysteries of the great "I am." The soaring wing must soar still higher. Our praise must only pause, to recommence its endless work.'[1]

God also uses the name 'God,' which translates the Hebrew word 'Elohim.' This word refers to God as the all-powerful Creator. Henry Law says of this word: 'This speaks of power and strength. It claims unbounded sovereignty.'[2]

All we have to do to be reminded of the grandeur of the God with whom we are dealing is look at creation.

The word 'Elohim' is also a plural. This reminds us that God consists of three persons, and all three were involved in the work of creation.

How can God be one God and yet be three persons? We cannot fully understand, but we do not have to understand in order for it to be true. And the Bible assures us that it is true. While the Bible does not give us a full explanation of the doctrine of the Trinity, it frequently asserts it.

The proclamation of God's goodness (vv.6b-7)

Having given Moses his names, God proceeds to reveal something of his goodness.

When Moses asked to see God's glory, he may very well have been thinking in terms of some kind of spectacle. We can be sure that the sight of the back parts of God would have been spectacular enough.

But God put more emphasis on his goodness. In doing so, he was essentially saying to Moses: 'You don't need to see a spectacle as much as you need to know my heart of love.'

To reveal his heart of love to Moses, God used the words 'merciful,' 'gracious,' 'longsuffering,' 'goodness,' and 'truth.'

♦ God is merciful. Henry Law defines mercy as '... that sweet
and tender love which has a tear for all distress, which grieves
in grief, and sorrows in sorrow, and yearns over all misery,
and only lives in healing wounds, and calming anguish, and
converting sighs to joy.'[3]

♦ God is gracious. Grace is his disposition to freely show mercy although there is nothing in those he loves to commend
them to him.

♦ God is longsuffering. He puts up with unworthy, undeserv-
ing people for a long time. He is slow to anger.

♦ God is good. The Hebrew word translated 'goodness' has to
do with God's faithfulness to his covenant and his devotion
to his people.

♦ God is true. He is faithfully devoted to his people because
he has promised to be, and he always keeps his promises.

After listing these attributes, God pointed Moses to the primary
manifestation of his goodness, that is, in the forgiveness of sins. He used
three words for sin: iniquity, transgression and sin. What terrible words!
'Iniquity' emphasizes the vileness and twistedness of sin. 'Transgression'
emphasizes the rebelliousness of sin. It violates God's law. And the word
'sin' carries the idea of failing to conform to God's standards.

But human sin is not larger than the mercy of God. How large is his
mercy? God forgives sinners by the 'thousands' (v.7). Henry Law says:
'O my soul, hearken to the melody of this sweet note. The thought may
sometimes rise, that mercy visits but a favoured few, that the rare gift en-
riches but rare souls. Nay, mercy's arms are very wide. Mercy's heart is very
large. Mercy's mansions are very many. It has brought saving joy to countless multitudes. It has saving joy for countless yet. The doors stand open.
Thousands have found. But there are stores for thousands yet.'[4]

While God's assurance of mercy are comforting and cheering beyond
measure, many find themselves troubled about what he added regarding

not clearing the guilty and visiting the iniquity of the fathers upon their children even to the third and fourth generation (v.7).

It almost seems as if God was giving something with one hand and taking it away with the other.

Why, then, does God add the words of verse 7? One reason was to underscore the seriousness of sin. When sinners hear about the mercy of God, they have a tendency to minimize sin.

How serious is sin? It is this serious – the consequences of it can linger long after we are gone!

By adding the words of verse 7, he also showed his love to be holy and just. God does not show mercy to sinners by either ignoring their sins or compromising with them. The phrase 'by no means clearing the guilty' means that God does not forgive sinners apart from dealing with their sins. He does not forgive sinners until their sins have been punished.

This, of course, puts us on good gospel ground. The glory of the gospel is that God clears sinners on the basis of Christ dying on their behalf and in their stead.

What happened when Jesus died on the cross? The Bible tells us that he received in the place and stead of sinners the punishment for their sins. He received an eternity's worth of wrath for them. This was necessary because God's justice demands that the penalty for sins be paid.

But God's justice only demands that the penalty be paid once. And if Jesus paid it for his people, there is no penalty left for them. God can and does clear them, then, because of what Jesus did. He does not clear them while they are still guilty of sin, but he transfers or imputes their guilt to Christ and clears them. Cheering thought!

Having looked at this wonderful proclamation from God, we are not at all surprised to read that 'Moses made haste and bowed his head toward the earth, and worshipped' (v.8).

The more we understand about the name of God and the goodness of God, the more inclined we will be to take our places alongside Moses.

Exodus 34:29-35

This may very well be the least surprising of all Scriptures. After having gotten a glimpse of the Lord and hearing him proclaim his Name and goodness, Moses came down from Mt. Sinai with his face shining.

How could it have been any other way? A man who has been taken into closer communion with God than any other must reflect that experience in some way.

In causing Moses face to shine, the Lord was certainly honouring Moses and confirming his leadership before the people. He was also honouring the people. How blessed they were to have Moses as their mediator and to know that the Lord had accepted him in that capacity!

It must have been a sight to see! Moses coming down from the mount with his face shining with a heavenly glory! Some of us might even find ourselves inclined to think that we would like to have been there to see it.

Would you be surprised if I were to tell you that it would be a step down for us if we could propel ourselves back through time to take our place among those people? And I am not talking about it being a step down because of the loss of cell phones, computers and cars.

It would be a step down because the glory of Moses' shining face, impressive as it was, cannot begin to compare to the glory shining in the Lord Jesus Christ. And the people of God are already seeing that glory.

Let's explore this a bit by looking first at...

The glory of Moses

The verses of our text suggest several things about this.

A reflected glory

First, it was a reflected glory. The glory did not belong to Moses. It was God's. It did not arise from within Moses but only showed on his face.

An unrealized glory

Secondly, it was a glory of which Moses was unconscious. Moses did not realize that his face was shining until he learned it from the people (v.29).

This contains a significant lesson for us. Alexander Maclaren puts it in these words:' … you may be sure that the more a man is like Christ, the less he knows it; and the better he is, the less he suspects it.'1

We should look sceptically, then, upon those who are constantly parading their spirituality. True spirituality never has to be advertised. It always advertises itself. The truly spiritual person is occupied with God, not with letting others know that he is occupied with God. Because this danger is always present, we must be ever mindful of the words of the Lord Jesus about giving alms, praying and fasting in order to be noticed (Matt. 6:1-19).

By the way, just as the person who is truly spiritual will not be aware of his spirituality, so it is possible for the child of God who is weak spiritually to not be aware of that weakness. Samson stands as a lasting reminder of this (Judges 16:20).

A frightening glory

The next thing for us to notice about the glory of Moses is that it made the people afraid of him (v.30). The glory of God is such that the mere reflection of it makes sinful people extremely uncomfortable.

When Isaiah saw the glory of the Lord in the temple, he cried out:

> *Woe is me, for I am undone!*
> *Because I am a man of unclean lips,*
> *And I dwell in the midst of a*
> *people of unclean lips;*
> *For my eyes have seen the King,*
> *The Lord of hosts* (Isa. 6:5)

It was when Simon Peter saw the glory of the Lord Jesus Christ that he cried: 'Depart from me, for I am a sinful man, O Lord!' (Luke 5:8).

A veiled glory

Finally, the glory of Moses was veiled except when he was proclaiming God's word or meeting with God (vv.31-35).

The veil was also removed when Moses spoke in order to convey the divine authority of the message he was delivering. That message consisted of an explanation of the commandments of God (v.32).

The veil was removed when Moses met with God because there was no need for it in that setting.

Why did Moses wear the veil at other times? We may rest assured that it was partially due to his humility. But it was also, as the apostle Paul mentions in his second letter to the Corinthians, to keep the people from seeing the glory fade. (2 Cor. 3:13). The shining of Moses' face was not to be a permanent feature. It was a temporary indication of the very special period of communion with the Lord that Moses had enjoyed.

With these things in place, we can now turn our attention to...

The greater glory of Jesus

This glory surpassed that of Moses in every way.

An unreflected glory

It was not a reflected glory. The glory of Jesus was his own. It was the glory of God himself because Jesus was nothing less than God in human flesh.

It is a very serious error to think that Jesus lost some of his glory when he came into this world. He did not cease to be God when he came. He added to his deity our humanity so that he was at one and the same time fully God and fully man.

While he was clothed in our humanity, the glory of God could still be seen. The apostle John put it in this fashion: 'And the Word became flesh and dwelt among us, and we beheld His glory, the glory as of the only be-gotten of the Father, full of grace and truth' (John 1:14).

The transfiguration of Jesus serves as a striking illustration of this truth. Before Peter, James and John, the Lord Jesus appeared in his heavenly glory (Matt. 17:1-9). In other words, he revealed to them the glory that was always there. Charles Erdman offers this summary of the transfiguration: 'It is as if the monarch had been walking in disguise; only occasionally beneath his humble garment has been revealed a glimpse of the purple and the gold. Here, for an hour, the disguise is withdrawn and the King appears in his real majesty and in the regal splendor of his divine glory.'[2]

A realized glory

It was a glory of which he was conscious. The Lord Jesus knew he was God in human flesh, and that the glory of God was shining out of his life. He explicitly claimed to be God on more than one occasion (John 5:17-18; 10:34-38). On no occasion did he more emphatically claim this than when he spoke these words to Philip: 'He who has seen Me has seen the Father' (John 14:9).

A glory that need not be feared

It is a glory of which we need not be afraid. How grateful we should be for this! The apostle Paul develops this in 2 Corinthians. He says that unbelievers have, as it were, a veil over their hearts so that they are unable to believe in Christ. But believers have had that veil removed by God (2 Cor. 3:15-18). With all this in place, the apostle draws this triumphant conclusion: 'For it is the God who commanded light to shine out of darkness who has shone in our hearts to give the light of the knowledge of the glory of God in the face of Jesus Christ' (2 Cor. 4:6).

The Lord Jesus came to provide salvation for sinners so they do not any longer have to live in fear of God and in fear of condemnation. They can rather can rest assured that God is their father and can enjoy access to him.

The Lord Jesus accomplished this through his death on the cross. This is the reason that he came to this earth. This is the reason he added our humanity to his deity. Deity cannot die, but humanity can. Jesus came to die. The sentence God pronounced upon sinners was death. For Jesus to remove our fear and dread of God, sin had to be removed, and the only way for sin to be removed was for its penalty to be paid. Having paid it, Jesus took away any reason for his people to fear condemnation.

A permanent glory

Finally, we must note that the glory of Jesus is a permanent glory.

The apostle Paul tells us that Moses had an additional reason for putting a veil over his shining face. The glory that radiated from him was a temporary thing. So Moses also wore the veil to keep the people from seeing the fading glory.

Why did Moses not want the people to see the fading glory of the law? That law was supposed to fade! It was a temporary measure to point the people to Christ, and yet Moses is preventing the people from seeing its fading nature. So, again, we must ask why? The answer, according to the apostle Paul, lay in the hardness of the people's hearts. They had turned from God after promising to obey his laws. As an act of judgement upon their rebelliousness, God hides the temporary nature of the law from them.

We can be confident that God will have his glory with each and every one of us. He will either glorify his grace by saving us or glorify his justice by judging us, but no one will keep God from having his glory.

Paul saw in that fading glory a type of the whole period of time that Moses represented, the period of the law. That law was designed to point the people toward the coming Messiah. When the Lord Jesus Christ came, the law had been fulfilled. We might say it had faded away.

Many of the people of Israel misunderstood their own law. Paul says it became a veil over their hearts. They failed to see the temporary glory of the law and tried to make it permanent. Those who come to know the Lord Jesus have had that veil removed from their hearts (2 Cor. 3:12-18).

And Christ is not one step on the journey to greater things. The glory of Christ is never going to be replaced by greater glory (Rev.21:22-23).

27 | Will you not come and join us?

Numbers 10:29-36

After being delivered from their bondage in Egypt, the people of Israel journeyed to Mt. Sinai where they camped for a year. During that time they received the law of God, built the tabernacle and were organized for the rest of their journey to Canaan.

It had been a most eventful year with lots of ups and downs, but now it was over and the Lord was ready for the people to resume their journey to the land of Canaan.

The passage we are considering may seem at first glance to offer a very small and insignificant detail. A multitude of preparations were involved to get thousands of Israelites moving again, and these verses offer us a conversation between Moses and his brother-in-law, Hobab. In particular, Moses asks Hobab to join him and the people of Israel in their journey to Canaan.

We are not told why Hobab was with the people of Israel or how long he had been with them. But as the people of Israel are preparing to resume their journey, he starts packing to return to his home in Midian.

He no sooner throws his socks into his suitcase than Moses sticks his head in the door and says: 'We are setting out for the place of which the Lord said, "I will give it to you." Come with us, and we will treat you well; for the Lord has promised good things to Israel' (v.29).

Every Christian can identify with Moses' words. The Christian is one who has set out on a journey, and he is eager for others to join him in that journey. He says to his family members and friends, his neighbours and his associates: 'Come with us!'

If you are an unbeliever, this invitation goes out to you. You have heard it before. Please hear it again. We who are believers plead with you to accept it. We do so on three grounds.

The place we are going is glorious

Moses was talking to Hobab about the land of Canaan. This was the land that God had promised to give the people of Israel, and they were on their way to possess it.

Christians are on their journey to a far better place. Scripture refers to Canaan as a land flowing with milk and honey, but, attractive as it was, it could not compare to the land awaiting the children of God. That land is heaven itself.

What is this land like? The Bible tells us that it is a land of peace, provision and permanence. It is a land of peace because there is no sorrow, no crying, no pain and no death there.

It is a land of provision because there God perfectly and abundantly cares for his people.

It is a land of permanence because life there will never end. These lines from John Newton put it perfectly:

> *When we've been there ten thousand years,*
> *Bright shining as the sun*
> *We've no less days to sing God's praise*
> *Than when we first begun*

The land to which Christians are journeying is so incomprehensibly glorious that the apostle Paul was able to write:

> *Eye has not seen, nor ear heard,*
> *Nor have entered into the heart of man*
> *The things which God has prepared for those*
> *who love Him (1 Cor. 2:9)*

A second ground that we Christians have for pleading with unbelieving friends to journey with us is this...

The information about this land is reliable

How do we know that land is out there waiting for us? The words Moses spoke to Hobab give us the answer. We know because 'the Lord said, "I will give it to you."'

If Moses had learned anything during his eighty plus years of living, it was to depend on God's word. God had promised to deliver the people of Israel from Egypt (Exod. 3:20; 6:6; 11:1), and he had delivered them. To accomplish this deliverance, God had promised to send various plagues upon Egypt, and each plague came.

As the people of Israel were on their way out of Egypt, God promised to divide the Red Sea before them and to cause them to cross over on dry ground (Exod. 14:16). And it happened just as God promised. With these and other promises fulfilled, there was no reason for Moses to doubt the fulfilment of God's promise about the land of Canaan.

The God who fulfilled all his promises to Moses and the children of Israel is the same God who has promised to give heaven and all its glories to those who have accepted his salvation. Our hope for it and confidence in it rests squarely upon his promise (John 14:1-3; Rev.21:1-4).

But can the Lord's word be trusted? Of course it can! We have even more reason to believe it than Moses because we know of even more promises that have been fulfilled. The most impressive of all these fulfilments is the resurrection of Jesus from the dead. Jesus himself promised it on several occasions, and he fulfilled it!

Another reason we can believe that God will give us heaven is this – he gave us his Son. And when I say God gave us his Son, I am not talking only about Christ coming to this earth but rather about him going to the cross. If God would go to the extent of sending his Son to receive the wrath of God against sinners, we may rest assured that God will never stop short of giving heaven to his people.

The bottom line is this: those who venture in faith on the Word of God will not be disappointed. It is a reliable word.

We believers also urge acceptance of our invitation for this reason –

The journey itself will do you good

Moses encouraged Hobab to accept his invitation by saying: ' … we will treat you well; … .' I prefer the way the King James Version states it: ' … we will do thee good: … .'

The people of God journey to heaven together. In other words, God places believers in a family which we know as the church. No church is perfect, and if you are so inclined, you can find much to criticize and what appear to be good reasons for staying away.

But when you lay all the deficiencies of the church alongside the good that she does, the latter will always outweigh the former. Let's think of our own dear church. She has been appointed by God as the company in which her members are to travel to heaven. As I have said, she is not perfect. But think of the good she has brought into your life. A few years ago I tried to capture something of this good in these lines:

> … *she has nurtured thee and thine*
> *On solid Bible meat and good gospel wine.*
> *She has constantly called you away from lesser things,*
> *And bidden you to faithfully serve the King of Kings.*
>
> *Oft'times amidst life's fevered pace,*
> *She did your weary, tattered soul embrace.*
> *And when under the crushing load you did bow*
> *She reached out to soothe your furrowed brow.*
>
> *When your sorrow did multiply and abound,*
> *She did you and yours with prayers surround.*
> *She has gladly your cares and burdens owned,*
> *And made you know you were not alone.*

Edward D. Griffin encourages unbelievers to take up the journey to heaven by speaking on behalf of every Bible-preaching church: 'We will assist you by our counsels, we will cheer you by our sympathies, and employ for you our prayers. Our heads, our hearts, our hands shall be ready to assist you. We will do what in us lies to support you in affliction and to strengthen you in temptation. We will watch over you with a brother's care; will rejoice when you rejoice and weep when you weep. We will unite our counsels with yours against the common foe, and will stand or fall with you. We will clinch hands and together break through the thickest ranks. Together will we conquer and together will we reign.'[1]

Hobab was at first reluctant to go. The pull of his home in Midian was strong, and we are not told here that Hobab agreed. But the passage clearly wants us to conclude that he did because the next section begins with the phrase 'So they departed ... ' (v.33).

The reasons Moses gave him won him over. How about you? Will you not think about the heaven to which Christians are headed, the evidences they have for believing as they do and the satisfaction of the journey itself? And, having thought about these things, will you not do as Hobab did and cast your lot with the people of God.

Do not allow yourself to be deceived at this point – if you desire to 'set out' for heaven, you must take the route that leads there. You will not arrive there, if you refuse to do so. And what is that route? It is marked out so very clearly. If you want to go to heaven you must trust completely in the saving work of the Lord Jesus Christ (John 3:16,36, 5:24; 14:6).

We who are Christians will go to heaven without you, but we much prefer to go with you. Will you not come and join us?

Numbers 11:1-15

After having spent a year at Mt. Sinai, the people of Israel have resumed their journey to the land of Canaan.

We might expect this to have been a time of excitement and joyful anticipation. The people were on their way to possess the land that God had promised to give them.

Moses may have even allowed himself to think that the most difficult part of his task was over.

This sobering and sad passage indicates that there was little joyful expectation among the people, and Moses' problems were far from being over. After having led the people in a journey of only three days, he encounters the first in a series of rebellions, two of which are documented in the verses before us.

These rebellions were so serious that Moses cried out to the Lord in despair: 'I am not able to bear all these people alone, because the burden is too heavy for me. If You treat me like this, please kill me here and now—if I have found favor in Your sight—and do not let me see my wretchedness!' (vv.14-15).

We must be careful how we treat this passage. It is not enough to say that it is about the people complaining. Yes, it is about that, but it involves much more. Neither is it enough to say it is about the Lord chastening or about how crushing the burden of leadership can be. Yes, these truths are also indelibly written here.

But there is still a deeper issue – a bedrock issue. Among the people of Israel, there was a loss of conviction about their calling. And – alas! – Moses himself temporarily loses sight of his calling.

It is important for us to consider these matters because the danger of losing sight of our calling is ever-present and unrelenting.

The people losing sight of their calling (vv.1-9)

These verses describe two instalments of complaining. The reason for the first is not given, but it was of such a nature that it sorely displeased the Lord and led to severe judgement (vv.1-3).

The second instalment of complaining focused on the issue of food. The people were tired of eating the manna that God had been supplying for a year. They yearned for the foods they had eaten in Egypt. Some of those foods - leeks, onions and garlic - caused someone to observe that they must have been a very smelly crowd!

Yearning for Egypt! This is no small thing. S.G. DeGraaf says it meant they were rejecting 'their holy calling and were likely to forsake the covenant.'[1]

At this point they were more interested in being God's comfortable people than in being his called people.

Here is a vital spiritual principle – If we do not understand God's purpose, we will not appreciate his ways.

God's purpose for the Israelites included several aspects or features. It involved making them a people of faith, a people who did not love this world but looked forward to a better world through the redeeming work of the coming Messiah. It involved having for himself a people who bore his image and reflected it to those around them. It included possessing a people that so rejoiced in having him as their God that they gladly ordered their lives according to his laws.

Now with that manifold purpose, it was necessary for God to adopt a totally different strategy than if he had only been trying to make the Israelites comfortable. Leeks, onions and garlic may well suit the latter, but it took a wilderness and manna to achieve the former. But the people, not fully appreciating his purpose, failed to appreciate the wilderness and the manna.

If all this has a familiar ring, it is because we often repeat the error of the Israelites. While God's purpose for us is much the same as it was for them, we can easily slide into thinking he should make life comfortable for us. And when life is not comfortable, we can even find ourselves thinking that God has failed us.

If we start out with the wrong job description for God, we will inevitably find ourselves thinking he has failed. But his job description is not our comfort!

We keep wanting to make Christianity an easy thing that requires no sacrifice and no inconvenience. But Christianity is not easy. If it had been, the Lord Jesus would not have spoken of it in terms of denying ourselves and taking up the cross (Matt. 16:24), and the apostle Paul would not have referred to it as a warfare (Eph. 6:10-20).

By the way, we should not lose sight of the fact that the complaining about the manna stemmed from the 'mixed multitude' (v.4). These were people who had gone along for the journey without having the faith of Israel. They were not redeemed people. But evidently they had enough influence to incite grumbling among many who were truly redeemed.

This reminds us that not all who company with the people of God actually belong to the Lord, and it cautions us not to accept at face value every assessment we hear about the work of the Lord. All is to be tested by the Word of God.

Moses losing sight of his calling (vv.10-15)

In these verses, the spotlight shifts from the people losing sight of their calling to Moses losing sight of his.

As we study Moses' life, we must always keep our eyes peeled on the unique role assigned to him by God. Moses was the leader of the nation of Israel, but he was much more. He was the mediator who stood between God and the people. He spoke to the people on behalf of God, and he spoke to God on behalf of the people.

Because of Moses' special role, we must not think we have adequately handled these verses if we merely draw certain lessons of leadership from them. There are such lessons to be drawn. We can talk about the immense and unrelenting pressure on spiritual leaders. We can talk about how people will always be people. They will always think the past is better than the present. They often lose their spiritual momentum, and they are, as we have already noted, all too easily influenced by people who are not spiritual.

But while such lessons are true enough, we must go beyond them to the issue of Moses as mediator. This passage shows us a most unpleasant sight, that is, Moses rebelling against his role. He calls his role an affliction from God, an indication that he, Moses, had not found favour in God's sight (v.11). He further characterizes it as an unbearable burden (vv.11,14), and as being a nursemaid for a bunch of babies (v.12). Believing that he alone is responsible for satisfying their cravings (v.13), Moses prays for God to kill him and thus rid him of his misery.

We must not be too hard on Moses. We know all too well the stuff out of which he was made!

This account is not here to give us reasons to kick Moses. It is rather here to show us his frailty as mediator so we will look beyond him to the perfect mediator. There is only one true mediator between God and man – the Lord Jesus Christ (1 Tim. 2:5). Moses was, then, only a provisional mediator who could at best foreshadow Christ.

By thinking along these lines, we have put ourselves in position to receive this most comforting thought – while the sins of the Israelites were so enormous that Moses wanted to abandon his role, the sins of his people are never so large that the Lord Jesus Christ will abandon them.

S.G. DeGraaf is certainly correct in saying: 'There is only one Mediator who could fully bear the sins of His people—Jesus Christ. He always had something to say to God and could pray for His people even when confronted with their most horrible sins. How fortunate that we know of a Mediator who never fails!'[2]

In his despair, Moses cried out: 'I am not able to bear all these people alone, … ' (v.14). That was essentially a cry for the Christ who without fail says: 'I can and will bear these people and their sins.'

What a heavy burden the mediatorial work of Christ brought to him! There on Calvary's cross he shouldered the wrath of God in their stead. But the weight of that burden was not too much for him. Because he bore it, his people have eternal life.

Numbers 11:16-35

As we read the accounts of Israel's journey through the wilderness, we must constantly remind ourselves of the words of the apostle Paul: 'Now all these things happened to them as examples, and they were written for our admonition, ...' (1 Cor. 10:11).

The people of God today are on a journey through a wilderness to a promised land just as much as Israel of old. The wilderness through which we journey is this world. The promised land to which we travel is heaven itself.

Because our journey is so very challenging, it is important for us to frequently evaluate our progress. The above passage can help us perform this vital task. It suggests four questions that we need to often ask ourselves.

Can we believe when God speaks?

Nothing is more vital in our journey than believing the Word of God. God is our guide. He has given us clear instructions in his Word. But if we do not believe his Word, it cannot profit us.

This passage speaks powerfully to us about this matter. Moses has complained to the Lord about the heaviness of the burden of leadership (vv.11-15). This complaint was prompted by the people's unhappiness over the manna with which God had been feeding them and their desire to return to Egypt (vv.4-5).

God responded to these complaints by promising to give the people meat to eat (vv.18-20). And, to our shock and dismay, Moses responded to God's promise with scepticism (vv.21-22).

Moses should have known better. Think of all the signs and wonders he had seen. But he let the difficulty of his circumstances blot from his mind all those instances in which the Lord had proven his power and might.

The Lord answered Moses' doubt with these simple words: 'Has the Lord's arm been shortened? Now you shall see whether My word will befall you or not' (v.23).

The Lord was essentially saying: 'Moses, I have revealed time after time my arm of might, and you are now talking as if it had been cut off.'

God often asks his people to believe things that seem to be impossible. Noah is to build an ark. Abraham is to believe that he and Sarah will have a son in their old age. Elisha is to prophesy an abundance of food for a starving city. Ezekiel is to believe that dry bones can be turned into an army. And we are to believe that salvation comes through a crucified Messiah. On and on we could go.

Many are quick to heap scorn and ridicule upon us when they hear such things. And not wanting to be considered out of step, we Christians can scramble to explain away the miraculous elements of the Bible. Meanwhile God tells us to simply believe every word that he has spoken – no matter how unlikely many of those words may seem.

And let us never forget that we are also called to believe that the Lord's arm is not shortened. The times are so hard that we can fall into the trap of thinking that they are too hard for God. But this is what the devil would have us believe. Nothing – including these evil times – is too hard for God (Gen. 18:14). Let us believe that and act accordingly.

We will do well on our journey if we travel with implicit faith in the Word of God.

Can we be happy when God uses others?

The Lord specifically responded to Moses' complaint about the burden of leadership by promising to put his Spirit upon seventy elders of Moses' choosing (vv.16-17).

Two of these men, Eldad and Medad, began prophesying (proclaiming God's truth) in the camp while Moses was meeting with the others (vv.24-26). Joshua, who was undoubtedly one of the elders, was disturbed. He saw the prophesying of these two men as an assault on Moses' position of leadership (vv.28-29).

Moses saw the matter differently – and correctly! – and said to Joshua: 'Oh that all the Lord's people were prophets and that the Lord would put His Spirit upon them!' (v.29).

Moses had his eye on the main thing. It was not that he and his ministry should be furthered, but rather that God's cause should be furthered.

All believers should take Moses' example to heart. The Christian journey is hard and demanding without carrying needless baggage. And envying others is definitely needless baggage. Preachers especially need this word. How easy it is for us to be jealous of the man to whom God has given larger gifts and a greater ministry! We should rather delight in each and every ministry that is unusually blessed of God, saying with the apostle Paul: 'Christ is preached; and in this I rejoice, yes, and will rejoice' (Phil. 1:18).

Paul had it right. What matters is not me and my ministry but Christ and his glory. And if he can be glorified in giving someone else larger gifts and a larger place, I must not only be content but also deliriously happy. It is not the place of any preacher to quarrel with the ministry his master has appointed. It is rather the place of each minister to be faithful in his place, seeking to proclaim there God's message and not his own unhappiness!

Can we be thankful when God provides?

The promise that God made to Moses was fulfilled – as will be the case with all his promises! The quail came in abundance, and the people ate and ate and ate (vv.31-35).

All would seem to be well. The people wanted meat to eat, and the Lord sent meat. But in verse 35 we read: 'But while the meat was still between their teeth, before it was chewed, the wrath of the Lord was aroused against the people, and the Lord struck the people with a very great plague.'

What happened here? Why did the Lord send such severe judgement? S.G. DeGraaf offers this explanation:' ... as they ate those quails, they were not filled with shame and remorse because of their ingratitude and faithlessness. Instead they acted as though it was simply their due. Therefore the Lord's anger was kindled against them, while they were still eating!'[1]

We could give this portion of Scripture the title 'How to eat quail.' Most of the people apparently received the quail with awareness of how sinful they had been and with gratitude for the Lord's goodness. They were spared. But many, whom Matthew Henry calls 'the ringleaders in the mutiny,'[2] did not receive the quail in this way and perished.

Their graves in the wilderness (Kibroth Hattaavah means 'graves of craving') gave silent and solemn testimony to the danger of despising God and his gifts (v.20). Those graves, while probably long gone, speak from the pages of Scripture, telling us to take our pilgrimage with keen awareness of the God who travels with us. If we receive his gifts with gratitude, we honour him and make the journey easier. If we despise his gifts, we invite his displeasure.

Can we trust and be quiet when we don't understand?

Every Scripture that affirms the judgement of God poses a significant problem for many. Such passages make them wonder how God can be loving and good and send such severe judgement. Many are always ready to judge God for judging!

It is ironic that they allow such passages to lead them into the very same position that many of the Israelites occupied in Numbers 11, that is, the position of forgetting God's many acts of kindness and complaining about his ways!

We must quickly and readily admit that we don't have answers to all our questions about the ways of God. But we must not take that to mean that there are no answers. We always have the terrible tendency to think that we see the whole picture when we actually see very little of it. And we also have the tendency to think we know a whole lot more than we actually know.

Our journey to heaven will be much less challenging if we will learn not to vex ourselves with questions that are too difficult for us (Ps. 131) but will rest in knowing that a day is coming when all God's ways will make perfect sense and we will joyously say: 'He has done all things well.'

When we finally come into his presence, we will be amazed beyond words with the wisdom and glory of God, and we will be stunned to finally realize how little we understood in this life.

While we wait for that day, we would do well not to pronounce judge-ment on God but to frequently say when confronted with his mysterious ways: 'I cannot begin to understand.'

30 | Journey to jealousy

Numbers 12:1-16

God's people are on a journey from this world of darkness to a world of light. They are journeying from earth to heaven, from that which is passing and dying to that which is eternal. They are journeying from heartache and pain to eternal joy and bliss. They are journeying from sin to complete freedom from sin.

What a blessing it is to be on this journey! And it is all due to the redeeming work of our God in and through his Son, Jesus Christ.

Every journey has its challenges and difficulties. There are bumps and chuckholes in the road. Sometimes our travelling companions are irritating. And sometimes we stray from the main road and find ourselves on a side-path.

As the people of Israel were journeying from Egypt to the land of Canaan, some of their most important people journeyed down a side-path. What a sad and shocking thing! The people who take this path are from Moses' family! Here his brother Aaron and his sister Miriam take a detour and journey to jealousy. A squalid town! Her air is heavy with stench. Her waters are stagnant and foul. Her streets are rat-infested and dirty.

Satan, ever the enemy of the people of God, delights in taking them to jealousy. Have you been there? Are you on the way there now? May God be pleased to use Israel's journey to jealousy to keep us from going there.

The audacity of this journey (vv.1-2)

Think about it. Miriam and Aaron side-tracking the people of Israel! Both had been marvellously used of God. Miriam had led the women of Israel in God-honouring praise after God opened the Red Sea. And Aaron was the high priest of Israel!

Both also had plenty of reasons to hold Moses in highest regard, especially Aaron for whom Moses had interceded after the golden calf episode. But Aaron, apparently a man who was very easily swayed by the opinions of others, sides with Miriam in complaining about Moses. The focus of their complaining? The lesser reason was that Moses was married to an Ethiopian woman (which was not forbidden by God as was marriage to a Canaanite). The larger reason was that they believed they were entitled to equal billing with Moses and weren't getting it (v.2).

What audacity! In light of all that God had done through Moses! And in light of all that Moses had recently been through (Num. 11)!

There can be little doubt about the reason this account is included. The Holy Spirit, the final author of Scripture, put it here as a warning to all generations of believers because every generation and every believer faces the same threat – jealousy! Someone is getting more noticed than I! Someone's ministry is better received than mine! Someone has been given a higher position than I! How very easy it all is! And how very damaging!

Let's tell it as it is. When we are jealous of someone, we are essentially unhappy with God. It is God who gifts his people and who determines their roles and spheres of service. If we were in love with God to the degree that we should be, we would only be concerned about him being glorified – even if that requires us to have a smaller role and take a lesser place.

Bishop Joseph Hall speaks from the 1600's to say: 'That man hath true light, which can be content to be a candle before the sun of others.'[1]

The results of this journey (vv.6-10,14-16)

We can classify these results in two ways – what did not happen and what did happen.

Regarding the former, we note that Moses did not seek to defend himself or vindicate himself. That is the point of verse 3, which, by the way, was not written by Moses himself but added by a later editor (if Moses had written it, it wouldn't be true!). Moses as a truly meek and humble man simply let Miriam and Aaron complain without seeking to justify himself.

What, then, did happen? God stepped in! The walls between earth and heaven are very thin. God knows when his people are complaining. People who complain about someone often hope that it will not get back to the subject of their complaining. They would do well to remember that it always gets back to God and he does not take it lightly!

God speaking

First, God stepped in to speak. Here he calls for Moses, Aaron and Miriam to appear before him in the tent of meeting (v.4). There he makes it plain that the reason Aaron and Miriam were not getting equal billing is because, he, the Lord, had determined that Moses should occupy a unique place in the whole scheme of redemption. God calls their attention to the fact that while he spoke to all prophets (v.6), he spoke in a special way to Moses, that is, 'face to face' (v.8) and had even shown Moses his 'form' (v.8, see Exod. 33:19-23).

Why should it be this way? God determined it to be so! Was this fair? Yes, because God is sovereign over all and can do as he pleases.

God judging

Secondly, God stepped in to judge. His judgement took two forms. First, there was the withdrawing of his presence (vv.9-10a). Secondly, there was the visiting of leprosy upon Miriam (v.10b). Hall says: ' ... her foul tongue is punished with a foul face.'2

Finally, the progress of Israel was slowed. (vv.14-16). While the sin of jealousy belonged to Miriam and Aaron alone, it affected all the people. This is evident from these words: ' ... the people did not journey on till Miriam was brought in again' (v.15).

Let us learn from this that our sins have a detrimental effect on others.

All of this flowed from 'the anger of the Lord' (v.9). God's anger has all but disappeared from the radar screen of humanity today. We assure ourselves that God is so loving and kind he could not possibly be angry with sin. But while his anger may have disappeared from our minds, it has not disappeared from God. He is the same just God today as he was then. His justice means that he cannot be ambivalent about sin. For God to ignore sin, he would have to compromise his holy character and deny himself. This he cannot do.

The joy in the journey (vv.11-13)

God is able to bring good out of evil, and he brings good out of Israel's journey to jealousy. There is joy in the journey.

Where is this joy to be found? First, there is the joy of repentance. When the leprosy breaks out on Miriam, Aaron cries to Moses: 'Oh, my lord! Please do not lay this sin on us, in which we have done foolishly and in which we have sinned!' (v.11).

While Aaron spoke, we can be sure that Miriam heartily concurred!

The prodigal son learned about the joy of repentance. Like Miriam and Aaron of old, he strayed from the path of obedience and journeyed into sin. Again, like Miriam and Aaron, he learned that sin ultimately brings heartache and woe. After demanding his inheritance and spending it all in 'riotous' living, the young man hit rock bottom. In the depth of misery, he determined that he would go home and ask for his father's forgiveness. He experienced the true joy of repentance when his father gave him a warm and abundant welcome (Luke 15:11-24).

Repentance is still God's prescription for sin. The apostle John assures us: 'If we confess our sins, he is faithful and just to forgive us our sins and to cleanse us from all unrighteousness' (1 John 1:9).

Miriam and Aaron's journey into jealousy also shows us the joy of having a mediator. Moses, as we have noted time after time, functioned in this capacity for Israel. And he does so again on this occasion. Upon hearing Aaron's cry, Moses says to the Lord: 'Please heal her, O God, I pray!' (v.13).

In functioning as a mediator, Moses once again foreshadows the true mediator, the Lord Jesus Christ.

When his people fall into sin, as Miriam and Aaron did, God can and will forgive them – not because they are worthy – but rather because Jesus their mediator is worthy and because he pleads for them.

We have absolutely no access to God and no forgiveness for our sins apart from the mediatorial work of Jesus Christ. How urgently important it is, then, to come to him acknowledging our sins and asking him to be our mediator.

31 | A failure in faith

Numbers 13:1-14:10

It would be hard to find a more disturbing portion of the Word of God. A year after having been delivered from Egypt, the people of Israel arrive at the border of the land of Canaan. All seemed to be in place for them to triumphantly possess the land, but they failed to enter.

These chapters are often preached when pastors are trying to lead their churches into a building or a relocation program. On such occasions, the program is likened to the land of Canaan waiting to be entered, and the people are urged not to fail as the Israelites did.

But this passage deals with an issue that is of daily importance for the people of God – living in faith! And what is faith? It is very often equated with positive thinking. We are told to select something – anything! – we want, and we shall have it if we do not doubt that it will be ours.

But biblical faith is a far cry from mere positive thinking. It is believing that which God has promised. We can and should believe what God has said because he, the object of our faith, is utterly trustworthy and reliable. In addition to telling us that God cannot lie (Num. 23:19; Titus 1:2; Heb. 6:18), Scripture holds before us many examples of his unfailing faithfulness.

Pastors who use this passage to build support for building programs would do well to consider while their programs may be good and needed, their success is not necessarily promised by God!

The failure of Numbers 13 and 14 is definitely a failure in faith. God had promised to give the people of Israel the land of Canaan, but most of the people refused to believe.

Unbelief is on display time after time in these chapters.

The sending of the spies

This was in and of itself a failure to believe. Yes, God told Moses to send men 'to spy out the land of Canaan' (13:1), but this evidently came after the people insisted that spies be sent (Deut. 1:22).

In telling Moses to send the spies, God was humouring the people. How patient and longsuffering he is!

What need was there of spies when God himself had already promised to give them the land? There is no small amount of irony in God's words: 'Send men to spy out the land of Canaan, which I am giving to the children of Israel; …' (13:1).

It appears that God is showing Moses the folly of sending the spies even while he is commanding that they be sent.

Does this not speak to us about wanting to subject much of the Word of God to human wisdom? We have in the Bible a divine revelation. Yes, it says things that are hard to understand and difficult to believe, but we are called to believe just the same. Many, aware of the difficulties and feeling the pressure of society, bring their wisdom to the Word of God and try to make it square with the popular notions of the day.

The report of the spies

Unbelief is also on display in these chapters when the spies returned to give their report. Ten of the spies gave 'a bad report' (13:32). They brought back some of 'the fruit of the land' (13:26), which proved it was indeed a land flowing 'with milk and honey' (13:27). But they quickly added that it would be impossible for Israel to possess it. The cities were strongly fortified and included many giants (13:28,31-33). Their pessimistic assessment was that this land devoured its inhabitants (13:32).

The implication was that the people of Israel would not be able to hold the land even if they conquered it. S.G. DeGraaf writes of Canaan: 'Because it was unusually fertile, the groups of inhabitants were continually battling one another for possession of it. And time and again they were attacked by foreign conquerors. Possessing that land was just too dangerous.'[1]

Joseph Hall summarizes the report of the ten in this graphic way: 'Their shoulders are laden with the grapes, and yet their hearts are overlaid with unbelief.'[2]

While the majority of the spies were giving their report, Caleb chimed in with a radically different word: 'Let us go up at once and take possession, for we are well able to overcome it' (13:30).

On the next day, Caleb warned the people that the more serious danger facing Israel did not lay in the land of Canaan among the fortified cities and giants. It rather lay in their own hearts that were inclined toward disobedience. It was far better to have the giants of Canaan as their enemies than to have God as their enemy (14:8-9).

How are we to explain the difference between what the ten said and what Caleb said? Caleb saw the same fortified cities and the same giants. But he also considered something that the ten had failed to consider, namely, the power of almighty God.

If the sovereign God of the universe has pledged to fight for his people, it doesn't matter how big their enemies are.

In other words, Caleb was not content to look only with a physical eye. He also looked with a spiritual eye. God's people always have the same choice in their difficulties and hardships. They can choose to look at their difficulties, or they can choose to look at their God. Much of our success in life depends on what we choose to see. May God help us to make the choice of Caleb and the choice of the apostle Paul who said: ' ... we do not look at the things which are seen, but at the things which are not seen. For the things which are seen are temporary, but the things which are not seen are eternal' (2 Cor. 4:18).

The response of the people

Unbelief is also on display in the response of the people to the spies' report (14:1-10). How did the people respond? They 'lifted up their voice and cried' (14:1). Furthermore, they 'murmured against Moses and Aaron' (14:2). They even went so far as to say: 'If only we had died in the land of Egypt! Or if only we had died in this wilderness!' (14:2).

Let's get this straight. The people do not want to go into Canaan because they are afraid they will die there. So they wish they had died already! As if graves in Egypt were superior to those in Canaan!

The people even begin making plans to return to Egypt! (14:3-4).

To top it all off, they decided to stone Moses, Aaron, Joshua and Caleb (14:10).

We could understand the unbelief of the spies and the people if God had not repeatedly demonstrated his might on their behalf. It would be understandable if God had commanded them to take the land of Canaan and given them no reason to believe that they could do so.

But God had again and again proven his devotion to his people and his willingness to use his power for them. He had showered plagues upon Egypt. He had opened the Red Sea before them. He had sent them manna from heaven.

Unbelief certainly has a short memory.

What does this episode have to do with us? The connection should be obvious. The people of God in every generation are called to faith. We are to believe all that God has spoken in his Word, the Bible. We are to believe what it tells us about the nature and personality of God. We are to believe what it tells us about the way of salvation. We are to believe what it tells us about our responsibilities as Christians – and we are to faithfully discharge them. We are to believe what it says about the cause of God, namely, that it will not fail but will be fully realized. We are to believe what it tells us about the eternal glory that awaits us.

Faith is never easy, but there are times in which it is more difficult. Our age seems to be such a time. Verily, there are giants in the land. The forces of unbelief seem to be so many and so ferocious that we cannot possibly stand for our faith and hope to succeed in our Christian duties.

The calling upon us is the same as it was upon the people of Israel. We are to keep our eyes on God and not on the difficulties of this hour.

Things are not as they seem. God is working even when he does not appear to be. The gospel is achieving victories of which we are not aware. History is moving toward the end which God has appointed. The crucified Jesus will finally prove to be the sovereign Lord of eternity, as every knee before him bows and every tongue confesses. And the people of God of all ages will finally join together in thunderous praise before the throne, saying:

Worthy is the Lamb who was
slain
To receive power and riches
and wisdom,
And strength and honor and
glory and blessing! (Rev. 5:12)

Let us hold to our faith. Let us not lose our nerve. Let us live this day and every day with that coming day clearly in view.

32 | Three prayings

Numbers 14:11-23

Ten of the spies whom Moses sent into the land of Canaan came back with a gloomy, pessimistic report. As far as they were concerned, it was impossible for the people of Israel to conquer the land even though God himself had promised it.

Two of the spies, Caleb and Joshua, urged the people to believe God's promise and begin the conquest. But the people were in no mood to listen to them or even to Moses. They started making plans to select someone to lead them back to Egypt (v.4). To keep Moses, Caleb, Joshua and Aaron from getting in the way, they decided to stone them (vv.4-5,10).

The planned stoning was short-circuited by the glory of God appearing in the tabernacle of meeting (v.10). This dazzling display of glory temporarily arrested the people in their mad course, serving as a visible reminder of the God with whom they were in covenant.

There have been many dark days in the long history of the human race and the history of the people of God. This has to rank as one of the darkest.

This dark day was about to get darker. The refusal of the people to enter Canaan can be characterized as the darkness of unbelief. We must now add to that the darkness of threatened judgement. Upon seeing this cloud of glory, Moses went out to the tabernacle. There the Lord spoke to him these sobering words: 'How long will these people reject Me? And how long will they not believe Me, with all the signs which I have performed among them? I will strike them with pestilence and disinherit them, and I will make of you a nation greater and mightier than they' (vv.11-12).

The dark day was now darker! But it was not totally dark. How Moses shines on this dark day! After hearing God's sentence of judgement, he begins to intercede for the people.

The praying of Moses

The purpose or goal of his intercession was to secure God's pardon for the people. As we have noted, they were under the threat of God's judgement. If carried out, that judgement would mean their immediate extinction and the building of a new nation through Moses. This would not have constituted a violation of God's promise to give the descendants of Abraham the land of Canaan in that Moses was a descendant of Abraham.

But, as Moses points out in his prayer, it would have been perceived as a violation of his promise by both the Egyptians and the Canaanites (vv.13-14) who knew that he had sworn to give the land of Canaan to the Israelites (v.16).

Furthermore, it would have been construed by these same nations as a failure of God's power. They would say that he was 'not able' (v.16) to see the matter through. John Gill states the conclusion of these nations in this way: 'though he brought them out of Egypt, he was not able to bring them through the wilderness into Canaan; and ... though he had wrought many signs and wonders for them, he could work no more, his power failed him, he had exhausted all his might.'[1]

The conclusion Moses drew from these things was that the Lord should demonstrate his power once again by pardoning the people (v.19), and, by so doing, show that his grace was greater than their sin.

In making this request, Moses was asking God to be what he had already revealed himself to be, that is, 'longsuffering and abundant in mercy, forgiving iniquity and transgression' (v.18).

But Moses was not asking God to deny himself, that is, he was not asking him to forego his justice (v.18). In other words, he was not asking God to withhold judgement altogether but only to spare the nation from obliteration.

Moses' praying was effective. The Lord responded by saying to him: 'I have pardoned, according to your word; ... ' (v.20).

The pardon was, of course, from the sentence of immediate death. God did not free the people from his discipline, which he carried out by consigning them to wander in the wilderness for 40 years. During those years, every Israelite over 20 years of age, with the exceptions of Caleb and Joshua, died. In this way God raised up a new generation of Israelites who believed his promise and conquered the land of Canaan.

Our praying

Why did the Holy Spirit see fit to include Moses' prayer in Scripture? What are we to learn from it?

Is it not here to teach us something about praying? Moses' prayer was based on what God had revealed about himself, namely, that he was both gracious and just (v.18).

We are also to pray on the basis of what God has revealed. We are to pray for things that are consistent with his character and for things he has promised to bestow.

Further, Moses' prayer was based on a concern for God's glory. He did not want the Egyptians and Canaanites drawing mistaken and adverse conclusions about God. Do we have here the reason so many of our prayers are so utterly futile? Aren't many of us more concerned in our praying about securing our own comfort instead of God's glory?

Finally, Moses' prayer included the element of reasoning with God. Moses reminded God that his glory was at stake here, and he, Moses, drew a conclusion on the basis of this.

This element of reasoning with God has all but vanished from our praying, and our praying is the worst for it! God likes for his people to remind him of what he has revealed and to remind him of his glory and to urge him to take action based on these things.

How are we to put this kind of praying into practice? One way in which we can do so is in our praying for revival. We so desperately need a mighty moving of God these days! Let us, therefore, point out to God that his name is being besmirched, his people are being attacked, his gospel is being scorned. And then let us ask him to reveal his glory! An example of this type of praying is found in Psalm 10. The psalmist begins with these questions:

> *Why do You stand afar off, O Lord?*
> *Why do you hide Yourself in times of trouble?* (v.1)

He then proceeds to call the Lord's attention to the flourishing of evil (vv.2-11). With all that in place, he comes to this appeal:

Arise, O Lord!
O God, lift up your hand!
Do not forget the humble (v.12)

This is how we need to be praying for revival! We need to call God's attention to these evil times and ask why he seems to be content to stand afar off. We need to ask him to rise up. We need to remind him that the honour of his name is at stake.

It may seem odd to us, but in praying this way we please God. He likes this! He likes for us to plead with him to show his glory!

The sad thing is that so very few in the church seem to be praying along these lines. We see evil mounting up around us, and we start circulating a petition or organizing a rally. As long as we think our activities are sufficient for these times, we will not be urgently praying for revival. It is only when we come to the end of our devices and see that we are absolutely helpless, that we will be driven to pray. And when we are driven to truly pray, we can expect God to step in. Let us learn from the prayer of King Jehoshaphat when he and his people were facing the combined armies of Ammon, Moab and others: 'O our God, will You not judge them? For we have no power against this great multitude that is coming against us; nor do we know what to do, but our eyes are upon You' (2 Chron. 20:12).

The praying of Jesus

There is yet another thing for us to take from Moses' prayer on this occasion. We are to see it as a wonderful anticipation of the mediatorial work of the Lord Jesus Christ.

We often have trouble finding ourselves in these Old Testament passages, and we are left wondering about their value for us. Have you found yourself in this passage?

The Bible tells us that we all come into this world with a sinful nature. Because of that we are under God's sentence of death. That sentence is not mere physical death, as was the case with Israel. It is rather the sentence of eternal death or eternal separation from God.

All would be hopeless were it not for this – the Lord Jesus steps between us and the wrath of God just as Moses did. God forgives our sins and lifts the sentence of eternal death, not because there is anything in us to commend us to him, but rather because of the Lord Jesus Christ and his atoning death on behalf of his people. Jesus pleads that death as being sufficient for the sins of his people, and asks the Father to pardon them on the basis of it (Rom. 8:34; Heb. 7:25; 9:24). And the Father agrees and pardons. Alexander Maclaren well says: 'Jesus is the true Mediator, whose intercession consists in presenting the constant efficacy of His sacrifice, and to whom God ever says, "I have pardoned according to Thy word."'[2]

Numbers 14:24

How sweet and refreshing it is to draw a deep breath of fresh air after being in a foul, rancid atmosphere! How invigorating it is to shower after toiling long hours in mud and grime!

Our text is something like that breath of fresh air and that invigorating shower. To change the figure, we might say it is like a gem glistening in a swamp.

In the midst of this heart-wrenching account of unbelief, disobedience and rebellion, the Holy Spirit interjects this verse about Caleb.

It is possible to write an epitaph that perfectly captures someone's life. At this point in the book of Numbers, Caleb has several years to live. But the Bible gives us his epitaph in advance. He is the man who fully followed the Lord.

If someone were asked to write a caption to summarize my life or yours to this point, what would he or she say? What will our epitaphs be?

May God be pleased to use the example of Caleb to inspire us so that we will also be known as people who fully followed the Lord.

How did Caleb come to fully follow the Lord? Our text tells us he had 'a different spirit.' If we are to fully follow the Lord, we must have this spirit. What kind of spirit is this? What kind of spirit did Caleb have?

First, we can say Caleb had...

A spirit of faith

The vast majority of the Israelites had a spirit of fear. Thinking only of the giants and fortified cities of Canaan, they were convinced that they could not possibly conquer the land of Canaan.

Caleb, on the other hand, had seen the same giants and the same cities, but he knew that God had promised to give the people the land and that God had not broken any of his promises.

The spirit of faith is that spirit which believes God's Word even when it appears to be utter folly to do so. Noah had that spirit of faith when he built the ark. How his friends and neighbours hooted with laughter as he hammered away! But Noah believed God's Word, and God's Word proved to be true.

Abraham was called to believe that he would be the father of a nation even though he was an old man and did not have any male descendant. The thing seemed impossible, but Abraham 'believed in the Lord' (Gen. 15:6). And, of course, the promise came true.

A young Jewish maiden was told that she would bear a son who would be conceived by the power of the Holy Spirit and apart from natural generation, and that young woman, Mary, believed God (Luke 1:26-38,45), and Jesus was born.

The spirit of faith, then, is the spirit that says with the apostle Paul: 'I believe God that it will be just as it was told me' (Acts 27:25).

It is the spirit that says with the man who came to Jesus with his demon-possessed son: 'Lord, I believe; help my unbelief!' (Mark 9:24).

Nothing is more urgently needed among the people of God than this spirit of faith. All God's people have faith, but faith can be great or small. The need is for great faith.

The church is so impressed and infatuated with modern thinking that she continues to concede huge amounts of territory without resistance. Evolutionary teaching comes along, and the church abandons the biblical teaching on creation. Pluralism comes along, and the church abandons the exclusivity of Christ and his salvation. The desire for entertainment comes along, and the church abandons biblical worship.

The church is so terribly afraid of being out of step with society that she gives no thought to the sad consequences of being out of step with God.

May God give us such a sweeping revival that the spirit of faith will seize us to the point that we will say: ' ... we also believe and therefore speak' (2 Cor. 4:13)!

This is sorely needed because much of the church today seems to be saying: 'We also doubt, and, therefore, do not know what to say.'

Caleb also had...

A spirit of obedience

If we have the spirit of faith, we must have the spirit of obedience. Why? Because commands are included in God's Word. If we believe that word, we must obey those commands.

The people of Israel had a spirit of rebellion and disobedience. Upon hearing 'the bad report of the land' given by the ten spies (v.36), they were ready to pack up and head back to Egypt (v.4), the will of God notwithstanding. Years later, Moses, in his review of the situation, would say: ' ... you would not go up, but rebelled against the command of the Lord your God; ... ' (Deut. 1:26)

But Caleb had a spirit of obedience. He, along with Joshua, pleaded with the people to not rebel against the Lord (v.9).

Do we have the spirit of Israel or the spirit of Caleb? The Lord leads his people 'in the paths of righteousness' (Ps. 23:3). Therefore, we cannot follow the Lord if we are not walking righteously.

And what does it mean to walk righteously? It is walking in compliance with or conformity to the Word of God.

To those who think they can follow the Lord while playing fast and loose with his commandments, the Lord Jesus himself says: 'But why do you call Me "Lord, Lord," and do not do the things which I say?' (Luke 6:46).

Hear him again as he says: 'If you love Me, keep My commandments' (John 14:15).

Finally, Caleb had...

A spirit of gratitude

The refusal of the people of Israel to enter the land of Canaan was nothing less than sheer ingratitude.

Think about all the Lord had done for these people. He had delivered them from cruel and oppressive bondage in Egypt. He had miraculously opened the Red Sea. He had fed them with bread from heaven. He had supplied water for them from a rock. He had established his covenant with them. He had patiently endured their murmuring and complaining.

But with all these blessings – and a thousand more! – they refused to do as God wanted. It was base, shocking ingratitude. There is nothing else to call it.

We are called to fully follow the Lord as were the Israelites. And we have many, many incentives for doing so. The Lord has so very abundantly blessed us. The grandest of all these blessings is, of course, salvation through the redeeming work of the Lord Jesus Christ.

Think for a moment about that wondrous work. We are saved because Jesus fully did that work. He did not take half-measures with it. He was fully devoted to it. He fully kept the law of God and, in doing so, provided the righteousness we lack. On the cross, he fully drained the cup of God's wrath, leaving not even a drop for those who believe. Jesus did redemption's work so fully and completely that he cried from the cross: 'It is finished!' (John 19:30).

Aren't you glad, brother or sister in Christ, for the fullness of Christ's work? Do you not love him for it? And is it not the desire of your heart to fully follow him?

All of the Lord's people follow him (John 10:27), but it is possible to not follow as fully as we ought. Let us ponder Calvary's work long enough and deeply enough that our hearts will yearn to take our place alongside Caleb in fuller fellowship.

Because Caleb followed the Lord while others were turning away, he was given the promise that he would finally enter the promised land. Forty long years came and went, and during those years Caleb spent a lot of his time going to funerals. When all the unbelieving Israelites died, only Caleb and Joshua remained. And Caleb, at age 85, realized the promise.

All those who follow the Lord will finally receive a far better inheritance – the promised land of heaven. With that land in view, let us give ourselves to fully following. When we fail, let's remember God's grace and try again. Let us keep following, no matter what others do, until we receive that good land.

31 | Three truths from a tough time

Numbers 14:26-45

This is a passage for us. It sets forth lessons that glisten and gleam as the noonday light, lessons that are just as important now as they were when the people of Israel first learned them.

The first of these lessons is...

Don't take lightly God's Word

This is exactly what the people of Israel did. God had commanded them to take possession of the land of Canaan, that land which he had promised to give them. Yes, they would have to fight to take it, but God had promised to give them the victory.

Those people refused to accept God's Word. Consulting their own wisdom and relying on the same, they set aside God's Word. They thought they knew better than God.

This is no small thing. God is very serious about this matter of his people believing his Word. How serious is he? Consider the following:

> ✦ He calls them an 'evil congregation' (vv.27,35). It is an evil thing – a wicked, malignant, depraved thing – to reject God's Word.

> ✦ He regards unbelief as being an assault upon himself. He says that the people were murmuring against him (v.27) and that they were 'gathered together' against him (v.35).

✦ He announces that they will wander in the wilderness for forty years, one year for each day that the spies scouted out the land of Canaan. During those years, every Israelite over the age of 20 would die with the exceptions of Joshua and Caleb, the two spies who urged the people to take the land.

Most of us have heard about the wilderness wanderings of the people of Israel for years. Do we appreciate their significance? Think for a moment about what these people could have experienced and enjoyed. They could have seen God giving them victory after victory. They could have rejoiced with each victory in knowing that God is powerful and that he is faithful to his promises. They could have enjoyed living in the land, having its bounty as their own. They could have enjoyed telling their children about God and urging them to live for him.

But they threw it all overboard to wander in the wilderness. Those years unite their separate voices to speak one word very loudly – 'loss.' The people of God lost out on many blessings because they refused to believe God.

God has given us a Word to believe as certainly as he did them. We have that Word in the Bible. Often, we find it very difficult to believe. We live in cultures that assure us that we are fools to accept this Word and to seek to live on the basis of it. Even many who profess to be Christians have abandoned faith in the Word of God.

But we must be willing to be in the minority, as Joshua and Caleb were, if being in the majority means forsaking God's Word. And we must always remember the lesson taught by the 40 years in the wilderness: We forfeit God's blessings when we refuse to obey his Word.

This principle has immense relevance for both believers and unbelievers. God's people rob themselves of spiritual power, spiritual peace and spiritual influence by doubting God's word.

And what about unbelievers? What do they forfeit by their unbelief? The Bible promises forgiveness of sins, adoption into God's family and eternal glory to all those who will forsake their sins and trust the Lord Jesus Christ as their Saviour.

But those who refuse to believe forfeit all these things – and more!

These are such unspeakably attractive blessings. Why would anyone refuse to receive them? The answer is, of course, that men and women today are not essentially different than they were in Moses' day. They are still so very sure of themselves. They think they know better than God. They would rather believe the latest opinion poll than believe the Bible. They refuse to believe that they are sinners. And if someone convinces them of their sinfulness, they insist on thinking that it is not serious. And if someone should convince them that it is serious, they refuse to believe that a man dying on a cross over two thousand years ago could have anything to do with the forgiveness of their sins.

The Israelites rise from the pages of Scripture to sound a solemn warning to believers and unbelievers alike. They tell us that we do not know better than God, that we must believe his word even when it seems outmoded, outdated and utterly absurd.

As we comb through this passage of Scripture, we discover yet another vital truth...

Don't give up easily on God's plans (v.31)

The last half of Numbers 14 may seem to be such a scene of unrelieved gloom that we find ourselves depressed as we read it. But all is not gloom and darkness. God loves to put shafts of light into dark episodes in Scripture. We have one such shaft in these words: 'But your little ones, whom you said would be victims, I will bring in, and they shall know the land which you despised' (v.31).

What a cheering word! The wilderness wanderings of the people of Israel did not mean the defeat or the overthrow of God's plan. God had promised that he would bring the people of Israel into the land of Canaan, and that is exactly what he would do. The very children they thought would die in attempting to conquer Canaan would in fact conquer it themselves. His plan could not be thwarted by their unbelief.

How we need this bright and sparkling word! It often looks as if the cause of God is going to come crashing to the ground. The increasing wolfishness of the devil's wolves and the increasing sheepishness of the Lord's sheep make it appear as if Christianity is going to perish from the face of the earth. We may frequently be inclined to think that the death rattle is in the throat of Christianity.

It is always too early to give up on God. History is filled with instances of the vultures of scepticism gliding with eager anticipation over Christianity, expecting to gorge themselves on its corpse, only to find that it was not dead!

How can we be sure the cause of Christ will not fail? If we look at Christ's fallible, weak people, we will find reason to tremble. But the cause of Christ rests, not on Christ's people, but on Christ himself. It is he who said: ' … on this rock, I will build My church, and the gates of Hades shall not prevail against it' (Matt. 16:28).

Genesis 3:15 shows history to consist of the struggle between the seed of the woman, Jesus, and the serpent, Satan. But the outcome of the struggle is not in doubt. The seed of the woman crushes the head of the serpent (Rom. 16:20).

That brings us to a final lesson from these verses:

Don't run presumptuously ahead of God

After hearing God's sentence of judgement upon their unwillingness to take the land, some of the people decided to reverse their course and launch an invasion. God told them not to undertake this, but, again thinking they knew better than God, they proceeded. It is not surprising that they met with disaster (vv.39-45).

These Israelites were guilty again of thinking they knew better than God. They refused to take the land when God told them to take it, and they tried to take it when God told them not to take it.

We also run ahead of God when we do things that he has not commanded us to do. God has given us work to do and has given us certain ways in which to do that work. The work is spiritual work and it must be done in a spiritual way. But many Christians use the arm of the flesh to fight the battles of the Lord. They perceive the cause of God to be growing weaker and evil to be increasingly militant. Something must be done! So they send around a petition. They organize politically. They pass resolutions. They bring into worship things not sanctioned by the Word of God.

How very often we Christians are like Simon Peter in the Garden of Gethsemane. He failed to do what Jesus commanded him to do – watch and pray – but then did what Jesus had not commanded him to do – attack with the sword.

The pressing need for the church in these days is to lay down the sword of human wisdom and effort and give herself to prayer. If we fight in Saul's armour, we will most certainly lose. If, like David, we go out in the power of God's Spirit, we will prevail.

It's always foolish to know more than God. It's always too early to give up on God. It's always painful to run ahead of God. These are some of the valuable lessons for us to learn from this passage.

Numbers 16:1-14

The people of Israel have turned away from the land of Canaan to wander in the wilderness until God raised up a new generation. We might expect these chastised people to have a new spirit. Perhaps some did. But the spirit of rebellion that caused the people to spurn the land of Canaan manifests itself again in this passage.

Korah, a cousin of Moses, evidently began a whispering campaign against Moses. This campaign succeeded to the extent that he was able to number 250 leaders of the congregation in his corner. John Calvin characterized these men as having a reputation which 'might dazzle the eyes of the simple.'[1]

Included in this number were Dathan, Abiram and On (v.1). The fact that we read no more regarding the latter may indicate that he repented shortly after joining these men.

With these men in tow, Korah approached Moses. I suggest that we approach this passage by looking at the people who are in this passage. Korah and his followers are here. Moses is here. And, yes, you and I are here as well.

The rebellion of Korah (vv.1-3,12-13)

What was Korah's problem? He was apparently unhappy that Moses' own brother, Aaron, had been selected as high priest instead of himself. And Korah's supporters (from the tribe of Reuben - v.1) were evidently unhappy that the tribe of Judah had, in the words of Matthew Henry, 'the first post of honour in the camp.'[2]

So the real reason for Korah's unhappiness was jealousy. But, not wanting to admit that, he pretended that the problem was the desire of Moses and Aaron for domination. They always had to have their own way! They took too much upon themselves (v.3) and exalted themselves above 'the congregation of the Lord' (v.3). Furthermore, Korah and his henchmen said 'all the congregation is holy, every one of them, and the Lord is among them' (v.3).

Their point was that every Israelite was just as capable of leading as were Moses and Aaron, and the reason leadership was not being passed around was because Moses and Aaron were power hungry.

The complaint of Korah and his supporters serves as another proof of a constant and on-going principle in human conflict, that is, the expressed issue is seldom the real issue.

We all know how this works. Someone gets unhappy with someone else, but the first someone, knowing deep down that he has no right to be upset or angry, pretends to be angry for another reason – a very high-sounding and spiritual reason!

The complaint of Korah is too comical and absurd for words. Moses and Aaron had not executed some sort of power-grab. They had not usurped authority over Israel. God had selected Moses to be the leader of Israel and had confirmed this selection again and again by doing mighty things through him. And Aaron had not been appointed high priest because Moses wanted to keep things in the family but because God had told him to put Aaron in this office (Exod. 28:; Num. 3:5-10).

Furthermore, it was a very odd time for Korah to be talking about how holy the people were in light of their refusal to obey God's command to take Canaan! Matthew Henry makes this point in these words: 'Small reason they had to boast of the people's purity, or of God's favour, as the people had been so frequently and so lately polluted with sin, and were now under the marks of God's displeasure, which should have made them thankful for priests to mediate between them and God; but, instead of that, they envy them.'[3]

Dathan and Abiram added more malicious words to those spoken by Korah (vv.12-14). They accused Moses of taking the people out of a land of milk and honey. How wonderful slavery was! They also accused him of failing to bring them into the land of Canaan and of 'acting like a prince' over the people.

The response of Moses (vv.4-11)

The way in which Moses responded to Korah and his followers shows his spiritual calibre. He first 'fell on his face' (v.4). By this act he registered his dismay that his leadership could be so misconstrued, acknowledged his helplessness and asked the Lord to graciously intervene.

Having apparently received the Lord's assurance that his prayer had been heard, Moses then spoke to the rebels. He first assured them that God himself would decide the matter on the next day (vv.5-7). The delay would seem to be for the purpose of giving Korah and his band the opportunity to repent.

In announcing this, Moses took the opportunity to turn their accusation upon them, saying: 'You take too much upon yourselves, you sons of Levi!' (v.7).

Matthew Henry writes: 'Those that take upon them to control and contradict God's appointment take too much upon them. It is enough for us to submit; it is too much for us to prescribe.'[4]

Moses concluded his speaking by offering a heartfelt appeal for them to re-consider their position (vv.8-11). He reminds them that God had already been abundantly kind to the Levites by placing them in charge of the work of the tabernacle (vv.9-10). The implication is that one should devote his attention to the work the Lord has given him instead of complaining about the work the Lord has given someone else! These rebels were so focused on the privileges of others that they had lost sight of their own!

Furthermore, Moses sought to show them the enormity of what they were doing. They thought they had gathered together to oppose him, Moses, but they were really 'gathered together against the Lord' (v.11).

Lessons for us

We have noticed the rebels' complaint and Moses' response to it. But what does it have to do with us?

I suggest that this incident speaks both words of caution and comfort to all believers in Christ. What are the words of caution? Here are some:

♦ the terrible danger of harbouring resentment and jealousy against a brother or sister in Jesus Christ.

♦ the pain and havoc that are created by actively campaigning against a brother or sister in Christ

♦ the danger of refusing to submit to the leadership that God has appointed for the church. One of the most grievous sins Christians can commit is to rise up against the leadership that God himself has ordained. With this happening so frequently these days, we have little reason to wonder why churches are so powerless and the gospel appears to make such little progress.

What are the words of comfort? One such word is for all spiritual leaders. This passage assures leaders that opposition will come. If it came to Moses, who may very well have been the best leader of all time, all Christian leaders can assume that it will come in time to them. Where is the comfort in that? It is in knowing that the same God who was sufficient for Moses in his situation will prove to be sufficient for them.

Another word of comfort emerges from these verses for all believers, namely, that God will always uphold his cause. Here we find under attack the head and mediator that he, God, had appointed over the nation. But God upheld Moses.

God has also appointed Jesus Christ as the mediator of eternal salvation and the head of his people. Many today are rising up in rebellion against Christ, but God will so uphold him that every tongue will finally confess that he is Lord of all (Phil. 2:11).

Let's think again about Korah's words to Moses and Aaron: 'You take too much upon yourselves' (v.3)

The very same charge is being laid against believers by many unbelievers. We claim that the Bible is the holy, inspired Word of God, and they say we are claiming too much. We claim that Jesus was God in human flesh, and they say we are claiming too much. We claim that Jesus' death on the cross is the only way for sinful people to ever stand acceptably in the presence of God, and they think we are claiming too much. We say Jesus Christ is coming again, and they charge that we are claiming too much.

But on the day to which Philippians 2:11 refers, it will be obvious to all that Christians never claimed too much for Jesus.

36 | A day of reckoning

Numbers 16:15-40

The day after announcing their unhappiness with Moses and Aaron, Korah and his followers, showed up at the tabernacle of meeting. They brought with them censers full of incense. The incense was a mixture of aromatic spices which was to be burned with animal sacrifices (Exod. 25:6). The censers were vessels in which fire was carried. When the incense was sprinkled on top of the censer, the fire caused its fragrance to be released.

Aaron, Moses' brother and the high priest of Israel, was also there with his censer.

All of this was in accordance with what Moses had demanded (vv.16-19). The purpose of all these people carrying censers was to resolve the issue placed before Israel by Korah and his followers, namely, whether Moses was to be the head of the nation and Aaron its high priest. If the incense offered by Aaron was acceptable to the Lord and the incense offered by the others was unacceptable, it would confirm that Moses and Aaron were the leaders whom God had appointed.

But simple confirmation of Moses and Aaron was not enough. Korah and his 250 followers had essentially spurned God and his covenant with the people of Israel. God would not tolerate this. We are not surprised, then, that the whole matter culminated with the ground opening to swallow Korah, Dathan, Abiram and their families (vv.27-34) and fire consuming the 250 who were offering incense (v.35).

Their day of reckoning had come.

Can there be any doubt about why we have this account in Scripture? Is it not here to remind us that a huge day of reckoning is coming?

Ours is a day in which people don't like to hear this. They try to ignore it, and they often ridicule those of us who believe in such a day.

But there is something inside each one of us that tells us it is true. A day of reckoning is coming. We can try to silence that voice. We can try to pretend it is not there. But it never quite goes away.

Let's take note of the major features of the day of reckoning in Numbers 16. As we do so, let us remember that these same features will be present on the final day of reckoning.

It was...

A day that revealed God's glory (v.19)

Korah and his company had no sooner arrived at the tabernacle of meeting than the glory of the Lord appeared.

This had happened so frequently during Moses' tenure that one cannot help but wonder how Korah and his fellow-rebels could have mustered the courage to oppose Moses (Exod. 16:7,10; Lev.9:6,23: Num. 14:10).

Did the sight of God's glory on this occasion cause Korah and the others to realize their error? Apparently not. The blinding and hardening power of sin is incomprehensibly great.

While much of what happened on that occasion is shrouded in mystery, it is clear that the final day of reckoning will make every creature fully aware of the glory of God (Hab. 2:14).

The whole issue between God and man is this business of God's glory. God created us for his glory. Sin is falling short of his glory (Rom. 3:23). And Judgement Day will reveal his glory to the extent that all those in rebellion will cry for the mountains and rocks to cover them (Rev.6:16-17).

While something of God's glory is apparent every single day of our lives, most people live without regard to it. On that day, they will no longer be able to ignore it.

That brings us to a second thing about the day of reckoning presented here in Numbers 16, namely, it was...

A day of separation on the basis of effective mediation (vv.20-23)

It may surprise us that God suddenly told Moses and Aaron to stand aside so he could consume the whole congregation (v.21).

Why would God threaten judgement against all the people for the sins of 250? We can well believe that God did this in order to set the stage for what happened next, that is, the mediation of Moses and Aaron (v.22).

Because of that mediation, God told the congregation to separate themselves from the rebels (vv.23-24).

While most of the people of Israel had not joined in Korah's rebellion, they were still guilty of sin and were deserving only of God's wrath, but the mediation of Moses and Aaron provided safety for them.

All of us who know the Lord should rejoice in knowing that the sentence of wrath carried out on the final day of reckoning would be ours if it were not for the saving work of the Lord Jesus Christ.

A third feature of the day of reckoning in our text is that it was:

An inescapable day (vv.23-27)

It is noteworthy that two of the rebels, Dathan and Abiram, refused to come to the tabernacle of meeting. But this did not exempt them from judgement. Moses came to them (v.25).

No one will escape the final day of reckoning. The apostle John was given a vision of that solemn day. He writes: 'Then I saw a great white throne and Him who sat on it, from whose face the earth and the heaven fled away. And there was found no place for them. And I saw the dead, small and great, standing before God, ... ' (Rev.20:11-12a).

John's words are plain. All of those who are dead in their sins will appear before God on the final day of reckoning. No one will be so small that he will escape detection. No one will be so significant and influential that he will be exempt. There will be 'no place' to hide.

Finally, we can say that the day of reckoning in our passage was –

A day which revealed the utter folly of the wicked

Korah and his people did not have to perish. It was utter folly for them to rise up against Moses. They had seen evidence after evidence that Moses was God's man. Moses was the one through whom God had sent plagues upon Egypt. Moses was the instrument which God had used to open the

Red Sea. Moses was the one whom God had designated to receive the law on Mt. Sinai. Moses was the man whom God had very recently vindicated when the people of Israel refused to enter the land of Canaan (14:36-37).

How much evidence did it take for these rebels to submit to Moses as their rightful leader?

We may very well ask that same question of all who reject the Lord Jesus Christ. God has appointed him as the only way of salvation. And God has given evidence after evidence that Jesus was indeed God in human flesh and the one and only Saviour.

Consider the miracles that he did. They were many in number. They were varied in character. They were observed by countless witnesses.

The most impressive of all evidences for Jesus is, of course, his resurrection from the grave. This proves beyond any shadow of doubt that Jesus is exactly who he claimed to be and that the salvation he came to provide is real and true.

And the resurrection is such a well-attested event that only those who are wilfully blind can refuse to accept it. The stone of the tomb was rolled away. The tomb was empty. Angels were present. The graveclothes were arranged in a convincing way. And hundreds of people saw the risen Christ.

What will you do with all this evidence? You can go through life ignoring it and rejecting it, but you cannot finally get away from it. When you finally come before God for the day of reckoning, you will realize how very foolish you were to spurn the Christ whom God appointed as the means of your salvation. But it will then be too late.

S. G. DeGraaf summarizes Numbers 16 in this way: 'Thus, for Israel's good, the Lord upheld Moses as head of the nation, but those rebels were forever removed from fellowship with that head and with that nation.'[1]

He then draws this conclusion: 'God also retains Jesus Christ as our Head, with whom we will be joined eternally in a glorious union. Breaking with Him means destruction and death. How many will be destroyed because they have chosen to break with Him?'[2]

37 | An old picture of on-going truths

Numbers 16:41-50

This passage is in the category of those that are often neglected and ignored. It's sad that this is the case. These verses are much needed in that they bring us face to face with the central themes of the Bible: human sinfulness, divine wrath and gracious atonement.

The reality of human sinfulness (v.41)

The deaths of Korah and his followers were obviously by supernatural means. The ground opened to swallow some (vv.28-34), and fire 'came out from the Lord' and consumed the others (v.35).

It should have been apparent to everyone in Israel that Moses was their God-ordained leader, Aaron their God-ordained priest and Korah and his band were Satan-ordained rebels.

With these things being so obvious, we expect to read that the people united around Moses. Such was not the case. Verse 41, one of the most shocking in the Bible, says: 'On the next day all the congregation of the children of Israel murmured against Moses and Aaron, saying, "You have killed the people of the Lord."'

Rebellion against Moses and Aaron had been severely judged, and the very next day there is more rebellion. This situation led Gordon Keddie to write: ' ... sin is not rational ... it is boldly blind to the inevitable results ... if you expect rational argument and the facts to change people, you can forget it. Sinners will sin on and just try to dodge the bullets!'[1]

Henry Mahan adds: 'This reveals the total blindness and hardness of the human heart. No amount of signs, miracles, nor witnesses will bring men to God apart from divine regeneration and revelation.'[2]

It is easy enough for us to see the sin of the Israelites on this occasion. The difficulty is in seeing our own. The largest challenge facing the modern day church is convincing people of the reality and enormity of their sins. No one will come to the Saviour until he sees himself as a sinner. Many in the church seem to be bent on offering salvation to people who see no need for it.

What, then, is our situation? Are we truly sinners? The Bible tells us that we are. What does this mean? It means refusing to conform to the laws of God. The reason people will not own themselves as sinners is because they go on the basis of their own feelings. They do not understand that sin is determined by an objective standard.

It is possible to be dreadfully ill and not know it. The doctor performs certain tests and tells us that we are seriously ill. We may very well respond that we feel well. But the doctor has in hand this objective evidence, and he tells us that it doesn't matter how we feel.

So it is in the spiritual realm. We feel that we are not sinners. But here is the law of God. It requires us to do certain things and not to do other things. It tells us that our compliance must not only be in an external way but internal. In other words, we are not only to keep these laws but to delight ourselves in them. How many of us can say that we have complied with all that God requires? How many of us can say we have never broken any of God's laws, that we have never had a wrong thought, spoken a wrong word or done something wrong? How many of us can say we delight in the law of God?

The fact is that we are sinners just as much the Israelites in this passage of Scripture.

But there is yet another parallel between that day and our own, that is...

The reality of divine wrath (vv.42-45)

No sooner do the people of Israel begin to murmur against Moses and Aaron than God himself steps in to threaten judgement. He says to Moses and Aaron: 'Get away from among the congregation, that I may consume them in a moment' (v.45).

Joseph Hall exclaims: 'When shall we see an end of these murmur-
ings, and these judgments? Because these men rose up against Moses and
Aaron, therefore God consumed them; and because God consumed them,
therefore the people rise up against Moses and Aaron: and now because
the people thus murmur, God hath again began to consume them. What a
circle is here of sins and judgments!'[3]

The only thing harder than persuading people of their sins is persuading them of God's wrath. If we press the issue hard enough, we can sometimes wring from those to whom we speak an admission that they are sinful. The problem then becomes convincing them that it is serious.

And why is it serious? The answer is, of course, the reality of divine
wrath. The Bible tells us that God cannot be ambivalent about our sin. He
is a holy God, and sin is an affront to him. His holy character requires him
to judge our sin. If he refused to do so, he would deny himself and compromise his own character. This he cannot do.

And what is the sentence God has pronounced on human sin? It is
eternal separation from himself.

So we have from this ancient episode a powerful reminder of human
sin and divine wrath. We should be grateful that we do not have to leave it
there. The passage also shows us...

The reality of atonement (vv.46-50)

No sooner had God announced that he would consume the people than
an unidentified plague began to sweep through them. Quickly discerning
what was taking place, Moses instructed Aaron to take fire from the altar,
put incense on it and 'make atonement' for the people (v.46).

Aaron did as Moses commanded. He 'stood between the dead and the
living' (v.48) and 'made atonement for the people' (v.47).

The word 'atonement' means 'the making of one' or 'to make at one
with.' The people of Israel were not one with God. Their sin had alienated
them from him. Before they could be at one with God, their sin had to be
dealt with or God's wrath against their sin had to be appeased.

The action that Aaron took provided atonement. It satisfied the wrath
of God against the sin of the people. It took their sin out of the way so that
they could be at one with God or at peace with God.

How did Aaron's action accomplish this? We must keep in mind that we have here the high priest of Israel coming between God and the people and offering incense to God. This satisfied God. We know Aaron's atonement was effective because we are told that 'the plague stopped' (v.48).

Gordon Keddie describes this atonement: 'There was no animal sacrifice here. Aaron was, in effect, the sacrifice. He was the advocate with God. He stood between the living and the dead, mediating between God and sinners.'[4]

This episode is full of meaning for us. It provides us a graphic and poignant picture of ourselves. We all need atonement. We come into this world in a state of alienation from God. Although we were made by God, sin has kept us from being at one with him.

And there is absolutely no way we can ever have that oneness until our sins are taken out of the way.

As Aaron made atonement for his people on that occasion, so Jesus Christ has made atonement for his people. He did so by going to the cross. There he stood between the dead – spiritually dead sinners – and the living God. He was on that cross in the capacity of the high priest of his people. He offered himself on their behalf. He received in his own person the wrath of God that was going out toward his people. In taking it, he exhausted it. He did not receive some of God's wrath so that his people would only have to bear the rest. He received it all so that they would have to bear none.

And as God the Father looked upon that cross and saw the flickering embers of what had been his holy wrath against sin, he was satisfied. That death was like sweet incense to him. His nostrils had been filled with the stench of our sins and the burning of his own wrath, but the death of Christ was like a soothing aroma to him. It replaced the stench. He smelled that aroma and was satisfied. This is why the apostle Paul wrote these words: 'Christ also has loved us and given Himself for us, an offering and a sacrifice to God for a sweet-smelling aroma' (Eph. 5:2)

Henry Mahan beautifully and powerfully moves from Aaron to Christ by saying: 'The people were dropping like dust as Aaron stepped between them and God to plead God's mercy for them. He was in effect saying, "Death and judgement, you must march over me and my atonement; you must smite God's high priest and ignore God's atonement if you destroy the people." Wrath and judgement have a claim on us. Justice is ready to smite the sheep. But Christ, the Mediator, stands between us and the justice of God and says, "You must walk over me and ignore my blood to destroy my sheep."[5]

Oh, what love Jesus had for his people that he would position himself as he did and receive what he did. How we should now love him!

38 | Encouragement from a stick

Numbers 17:1-13

This passage brings us to one of the most absorbing and astonishing events in the Old Testament, and, for that matter, in all of history. I am not calling attention to it because it is amazing but rather because it is profoundly encouraging.

The miracle of Aaron's rod was designed to put an end to the spirit of rebellion among the people of Israel. It was intended to silence the grumbling against the leadership of Moses and the priesthood of Aaron (v.5).

Each of the leaders of the twelve tribes of Israel was to write his name on his rod and present it to Moses. Aaron's name was written on the rod representing the tribe of Levi. All the rods were to be placed in the Tent of Meeting. God promised that one of these rods would blossom, and, in so doing, would indicate the man whom God had chosen to serve as his priest (vv.1-5).

All was done according to what the Lord commanded (vv.6-7). On the next day, Moses went into the Tent of Meeting. What a sight greeted him! Aaron's rod ' ... had sprouted, put forth buds, had produced blossoms and yielded ripe almonds' (v.8).

It would have been impressive enough if this dead stick would have just sprouted. But in one night it also produced ripe almonds!

What are we to take away from this startling event? I suggest that this rod produced far more than blossoms and almonds, that it also produced tremendous encouragement for the people of God in every generation. There is encouragement here for us.

What encouraging truths do we find here?

The first and most obvious is this:

God has the power to do the impossible

Let's do a little time travel. We climb into our time machine and it spins us around and spits us out right here in Numbers 17. We now see Moses taking those dead sticks into his arms. Someone sidles up and whispers: 'What do you think? Will one of these rods actually blossom?'

Would we not have been inclined to dismiss the possibility? Had we been there, many of us may very well have said: 'Dead sticks don't blossom. It's impossible!'

But God can do the impossible!

Here are Abraham and Sarah. God has told them that they will have a son. But Sarah is well past the age of child-bearing, and Abraham's body is 'as good as dead' (Heb. 11:12). One might as well talk about a dead man fathering a child as to talk about Abraham doing it. But God stepped into that impossible situation, and Isaac was born. And God proved that nothing is too hard for him (Gen. 18:14).

Over here are the people of Judah in captivity in Babylon. The situation seems impossible. Babylon is so strong. To talk about Judah being a nation again would make as much sense as talking about raising up an army from a valley of dry bones. But, as God showed the prophet Ezekiel, he, the Lord has the power to raise up such an army (Ezek. 37). This is the God who restored Judah to nationhood as he had promised.

And here is a young woman who is told that she will conceive and bear a son while she is still a virgin, and that Son will be God himself in human flesh. Many would say of that situation: 'It is a dead stick. It is impossible.' But the angel Gabriel said: 'For with God nothing will be impossible' (Luke 1:37).

That same Son is now being taken off a Roman cross to be placed in a tomb. Seeing that lifeless body, many would say a resurrection was impossible. It appeared to be a dead stick. But, oh, how God made that stick blossom! The Lord Jesus arose from that grave and lives today!

This is the same God with whom we are dealing today – the God who is sovereign over all. What encouragement this provides!

Some of you are dealing with seemingly hopeless situations. It may be that your son or your daughter has gone so far into some kind of addiction or into hostility toward the things of God, that it appears that there is no hope. You look at that son or daughter, and you find yourself thinking that this is a dead stick. God can make that dead stick blossom!

The truth is that every single child of God was once as dead as those rods that Moses carried in his arms. We were once dead in our trespasses and sins, but the God who breathed life into Aaron's rod breathed spiritual life into us. He found us in the spiritual graveyard and quickened us, that is, gave us life (Eph. 2:1-7).

Here is a truth that you can lay hold of when you are standing beside the grave of a believing loved one. The situation appears to be hopeless. Dead sticks don't blossom, and dead people don't live. But the God who made Aaron's rod blossom and produce fruit will send his Son, Jesus Christ, with the shout of the archangel and a blast from the trumpet of God. And the dead in Christ will spring from their graves to share in the glorious resurrection life of Jesus himself (1 Thess. 4:13-18).

Some of us look at the church today and see a dead stick. The devil and his forces are so powerful, and the church seems so helpless and weak. But there is such a thing as revival. And what is revival? It is that time when God breathes fresh life and vigour into the seemingly lifeless body of his church. Dead sticks can blossom!

The Israelites under Moses served as proofs of this very thing. There they were in bondage in Egypt. It looked as if there was no hope for them as a nation. But God had with a strong arm brought them out. Dead sticks can blossom and produce fruit!

A second encouraging truth for us to glean from the blossoming of Aaron's rod is this:

God will finally vindicate himself and those whom he has chosen

In rebelling against Moses and Aaron, the people of Israel were rebelling against God himself. Moses and Aaron had not usurped authority.

In making Aaron's rod blossom and produce fruit, God vindicated himself as well as Moses and Aaron. He both showed that he had the right to choose, and that in Moses and Aaron he had exercised that right.

The most obvious application is clear. Just as God had chosen Aaron to be high priest of Israel, so he has chosen Christ as the high priest of our salvation (Heb. 7:20-10:18). Those who reject him will finally see him vindicated as the only Lord and Saviour (Rev.4:1-5:14).

God still chooses leaders for his people, and he still expects his people to follow them. The author of Hebrews says: 'Obey those who rule over you, and be submissive, for they watch out for your souls, as those who must give account. Let them do so with joy and not with grief, for that would be unprofitable for you' (Heb. 13:7).

All pastors can take consolation in knowing that the same God who vindicated Moses and Aaron will finally vindicate them as well.

But there is also another point of application. All God's people are his chosen ones (Eph. 1:4), chosen in grace before the foundation of the world. Yes, salvation is this big – it reaches from eternity past to eternity future. And to be saved means being part of this vast reach.

To be saved also means encountering opposition and scorn (Phil. 1:27; 2 Tim. 3:12).

But God will finally vindicate his own. Here they are often cast into the mud of disdain and contempt, but God will some day gather them and cause them to glitter like jewels (Mal. 3:17). On that day they will shine as the stars in the firmament (Dan. 12:3). And it will finally be apparent to the watching universe that the people of God were wise to follow the Lord.

Walter Chantry captures something of that day of vindication in these words: 'Defeated foes watch in helpless ruin. Observing is the sceptic who once sneered that there was no reality to the Church's trust in this unseen King. ... All who preferred a fallen world system with its pleasures and riches will sit amidst the ruins and ashes of that temporary order now demolished. They will lift their shameful heads to see the Church in a gown interwoven with gold, all radiant in the presence of her loving Lord, about to enter his kingdom and hers. No doubt will remain in any soul of the wisdom of waiting for Messiah and the foolishness of having scorned his offers of mercy. But the Church will pass them by. At that moment those who are accursed will be accursed still. They will have forever to envy the Church and regret their tragic rejection of her society on earth.'[1]

Numbers 20:1-13

The name 'Kadesh' ought to ring a bell. That was the place where the people of Israel had refused to enter the land of Canaan (Num. 13:26).

Thirty-eight years have come and gone, and now the people are in Kadesh again. Little time was now left for those who were destined to die in the wilderness (Num. 14:26-35). Since Miriam, Moses' sister, was part of that generation, we are not surprised to read that she died at Kadesh (v.1). We would do well at this point to reflect on Gordon Keddie's words regarding Miriam: 'If we are inclined to think God harsh in thus depriving her of entrance into Canaan, we should remember that Miriam was a believer, dying at a great age and passing into glory to be for ever with the Lord.'[1]

While we are not surprised about Miriam, we must certainly feel a sense of shock about what we read next – the complaining of the people of Israel.

We have every reason to expect better. This new generation had seen their fathers rebel against God and Moses on several occasions with very unhappy consequences each time.

But the biggest disappointment in this passage comes from Moses and Aaron.

They began well, immediately going to the Lord about the grumbling of the people (v.6).

And the Lord told them what to do. They were to take the rod of Aaron which was kept there in the Tent of Meeting, gather the people around a certain rock and speak to it. And the promise was that it would produce enough water for the people and their animals (v.8).

All of this calls to mind a previous occasion when the people of Israel needed water (Exod. 17:1-7). At that time Moses was not to speak to the rock but strike it with his rod.

While Moses obeyed on that occasion, he failed to do so here. This reminds us that even men and women of profound faith fail and fail horribly. We never advance so far in spiritual things that we are beyond the reach of sin.

Filled with anger and frustration over the grumbling, Moses said to the people: 'Hear now, you rebels! Must we bring water for you out of this rock?' (v.10).

He then struck the rock twice with the rod of Aaron. The water came gushing out, giving testimony to the fact that God's grace is greater than our sin. But the Lord was so sorely displeased with Moses and Aaron that he pronounced judgement on them (v.12).

The Israelites received more that day than water. This event set before them some vital truths. I suggest that these truths are still in effect, that our success and happiness in living hinges on our learning and prizing these very truths.

The first and most obvious of these truths is this:

God takes disobedience seriously

Many find this to be a very troubling passage. It seems that God was unreasonable. Yes, Moses disobeyed, but what was the harm of it? What did it matter if he hit the rock? The people got their water. Was that not what really mattered? Was God not being unduly harsh about this business?

We will not draw such a conclusion if we keep certain things in mind.

The unique role of Moses and Aaron

First, we must remember the unique role of Moses and Aaron. Each of these men functioned at various times as the mediator between God and Israel. When they stepped into that role, they pre-figured the Lord Jesus Christ who had already been appointed by God the Father as the true mediator between himself and sinners.

An essential part of the work of the Lord Jesus Christ was perfect obedience to the laws of God. He could not have redeemed sinners if he had been one himself.

Moses and Aaron were not perfect men, but it was very important when they stepped into that role of mediator that they demonstrate obedience. On this occasion, they failed.

The time

We must also keep in mind the time that it occurred. The people were once again at the border of Canaan. The previous generation had failed to enter because of disobedience. This generation must now see once again the importance of obedience and the consequences of disobedience. They must see that even the leaders of Israel, Moses and Aaron, were not given a pass on this matter of obedience.

Ours is a time in which people are exceedingly casual about the things of God. People think if they give God a little bit of their time when it is convenient for them that they are free to live as they please. While we are becoming more and more casual about God's commandments, God himself has not changed. He still places a premium on obedience (1 Sam. 15:22; Luke 6:46) and assures us that we will eventually give account to him for every act of disobedience (Rom. 14:12).

It is interesting that God connected Moses and Aaron's disobedience with failure to 'hallow' or honour him (v.12). The point is unmistakably clear – if we want to honour God, we must obey him.

A second major truth that emerges from this account is this:

God takes unbelief seriously

God also connected the disobedience of Moses and Aaron with failure to believe him (v.12).

God had spoken to Moses and Aaron. He had instructed them to speak to the rock and promised that it would produce water (v.8).

When Moses struck the rock, he was essentially saying that God's word is not true. He was essentially rebelling against God's instructions and doubting God's promise.

This is the reason that Samuel calls rebellion or disobedience 'the sin of witchcraft' (1 Sam. 15:23). Witchcraft sets aside the revealed truth of God and seeks its own revelation.

Nothing offends God more than our refusal to believe his word. Every act of disobedience is, therefore, an insult to God.

A final truth suggested by this passage can be put in this way:

God takes his plan of salvation seriously

The apostle Paul tells us that this rock in the wilderness was a figure or type of the Christ (1 Cor. 10:4) for whom all believing Israelites were looking.

With this piece of information in mind, let's think again about the two instances of Moses striking the rock for water.

In the first instance, the Hebrew word translated 'rock' refers to a low rock (Exod. 17:6). The word translated 'rock' here in Numbers 20 refers to an elevated rock.

The rock represents the Lord Jesus Christ in each case. The lowness of the rock in Exodus 17 represents him in his lowly state, that is, when he humbled himself and took our humanity. The elevated rock in Numbers 20 represents the Lord Jesus in his current state, that is, his exalted state.

The fact that Moses was to strike the low-lying rock and speak to the elevated rock conveys powerful spiritual truth. It tells us that the Lord Jesus was to be stricken or smitten while he was here on earth in the flesh (Isa. 53:4-5), and that smiting would produce living, spiritual water that would quench the thirst and satisfy the soul (John 4:13-14; 7:37-38).

But Christ was to be smitten only once. To receive the on-going supply of spiritual water to sustain us we must now speak to the exalted Christ in prayer.

A.W. Pink writes: 'Streams of spiritual refreshment flow to us on the ground of *accomplished redemption* and in connection with Christ's *priestly ministry*.'[2] (italics are his).

The sin of Moses and Aaron was serious because it spoiled the type and misrepresented God's plan of salvation.

The conclusion for us to carry away from this is that God is very precise about the whole business of salvation, and we must be precise as well.

This runs counter to the mood of the age. While we love precision in other areas, we do not want it in the things of God. We want it in the natural order. We want night to follow day, and day to follow night. We want the four seasons to come in order. We want it in the medical field. We do not want the doctor guessing about our physical problems. We certainly want it in sporting events. We do not want the referee to call a touchdown when a player on the opposing team is still ten yards away from the goal line. But we do not want it in the area of salvation. There we want to say things like this: 'Everyone has his own view, and no one can say who is right or wrong.'

But there is someone who can say, and that is God. And he has spoken on this matter of salvation. He has clearly said that salvation is only through faith in the saving work of Jesus Christ. We ignore such clarity to the ruin of our own souls.

40 | A type of Christ

Numbers 21:4-9

One of the primary proofs that the Bible is the Word of God is the fulfilment of its prophecies and types. We know that a good part of biblical prophecy is the foretelling of future events. The Old Testament abounds, for example, with prophecies about the Lord Jesus Christ. His birth, death, burial and resurrection are all foretold with amazing detail. And all were fulfilled to the letter!

The Old Testament also includes types of Christ. A type is a person, an institution or an event that portrays some aspect of the person or work of Christ. Joseph and David are two persons who serve as types of Christ. And, as we have noticed several times, so is Moses!

The sacrifice of animals is, of course, the most significant of all the institutional types. This institution portrays the Lord Jesus Christ shedding his blood as a sacrifice for sinners. The temple itself is another example of institutional types.

The best example of an event that served as a type of Christ is the Passover. That event in Israel's history foreshadowed the work of Jesus who is the Passover for believers (1 Cor. 5:7).

We have in the passage before us another example of an event that serves as a type of Christ. Here the people of Israel are bitten by poisonous serpents, and Moses is instructed by God to make a serpent of brass and put it on a pole in the camp.

That serpent of brass is a type of the Lord Jesus Christ and his atoning work on the cross. There can be absolutely no doubt about this because the Lord Jesus himself made it clear in these words that he spoke to Nicodemus: 'And as Moses lifted up the serpent in the wilderness, even so must the Son of Man be lifted up, ... ' (John 3:14).

If Jesus said it, that settles it.

The lifting up is the main point of connection between the brass serpent made by Moses and the Lord Jesus Christ. But we can identify other parallels as well.

The parallel of sin

The sinful condition of the people of Israel at this time is an emblem or type of the sinful condition of us all.

Here we find the people of Israel falling once again into that sin that so often beset them, the sin of grumbling against God and Moses (v.5). The difficulty and hardships of the journey were real, and the people were deeply discouraged.

But discouragement with circumstances does not justify grumbling.

This grumbling is particularly disturbing because it comes after 38 years of wandering in the wilderness. Those 38 years were a testimony to the terrible danger of this particular sin. The old generation had almost completely passed off the scene for this very sin, and now the new generation, the one that was designated to conquer the land of Canaan, repeats the sin. It appears that these people have learned nothing.

What was the cause of their grumbling? It was the manna with which God had been feeding them. That manna sustained their lives. It was a manifestation of God's goodness. But they complained about it.

We tend to think complaining is not a serious matter, but it is. All grumbling is essentially an attack on God and how he is running things!

The sin of Israel on this occasion, I say, is a good representation of the sinful nature which we all have. We all rebel against God, refusing to do what he tells us to do. We all blame God, finding fault with him, his word and his servants, instead of admitting that our troubles are due to our own sins. We all complain against God, thinking that he should bless us more than he has.

The manna about which these people were complaining was itself a type of Christ (John 6:41,48-51,58). These people were essentially complaining, then, about the coming Christ and the salvation that he was to provide. How many today are not content with Christ as the bread of life! Instead of rejoicing in his salvation, many find fault with it.

The parallel of judgement

The judgement that befell the people is an emblem or type of the judgement that awaits all those who do not know God.

This judgement was both severe and just. The severity of it is evident from these words: 'the Lord sent fiery serpents among the people, and they bit the people, and many of the people of Israel died' (v.6).

The bite of these 'fiery' serpents must have been most dreadful indeed. It caused intense, searing pain, incredible anguish, suffering and death!

The Bible tells us that there is a fiery judgement awaiting all those who die in their sins (Luke 16:23; 2 Thess. 1:7-9).

This judgement was also just. God had enormously blessed these people and had long suffered with them and their sinfulness.

Many complain about the severity of the Bible's teaching about the wrath of God, but in due time it will become apparent that God's punishment of the wicked is eminently fair and just.

When the dust of history settles, no one will be able to find a shred of injustice with God. In fact, just the opposite will be the case. On that day, all will marvel that God was so gracious and kind and patient. On that day, what is now so often hidden from our eyes will be clear as the noonday sun, that is, what an enormously wicked thing it is for creatures to rebel against their Creator. And all will have to confess that such wickedness deserves the most severe judgement.

The parallel of the remedy

The remedy applied by Moses is an emblem or type of the salvation provided by Christ.

There are several things for us to note here.

First, the remedy did not come from Moses but from God.

Verse 8 says: 'Then the Lord said the Moses, "Make a fiery serpent, and set it on a pole."'

Salvation through Jesus' death on the cross is God's plan. It could be no other way. Sin has so affected us that we have no interest in coming to

God. And if we had the interest, there would be nothing we could do to save ourselves. Salvation is of the Lord (Jonah 2:9). God is the one against whom we have sinned, and God is the one who graciously desired to restore sinners to fellowship with himself. The means God chose is the death of his Son.

Secondly, the remedy consisted of Moses making a serpent in the likeness of the fiery serpents.

In like manner, God's plan of salvation consisted of the Lord Jesus Christ being made in 'the likeness of men' (John 1:14; Rom. 8:3; 2 Cor. 5:21; Phil. 2:7).

I say again that it could be no other way. The Son of God had to be one of us in order to do something for us. It was mankind that had broken God's law and incurred God's wrath. Mankind had to pay that penalty. For God to pay it on our behalf, he had to be one of us.

Thirdly, the serpent Moses made had no venom.

While the bronze serpent was made in the likeness of the poisonous serpents, it was not totally like them.

So it was with the Lord Jesus Christ. While he was truly one of us, he was not totally like us. He was without the venom of sin (2 Cor. 5:21; 1 Peter 1:29; 1 John 3:5).

Once again, it had to be this way. If Jesus had been guilty of sin, he would have had to pay for his own sins and could not, therefore, have paid for the sins of others.

Fourthly, as we have already noted, Moses had to lift the serpent up on a pole, and the Lord Jesus had to be lifted up on the cross.

It was fitting that Jesus should be suspended between heaven and earth because he came to conduct business between heaven and earth and to be, as it were, the bridge between the two.

Fifthly, all that was necessary for the people to be healed was to look at the brass serpent, and all that is necessary for healing from sin is to look to Christ.

To look carries with it the idea of trust. If I say, I look to a plumber to take care of plumbing problems and to an electrician to take care of my electrical problems, you would understand me to be saying that I depend on these people and trust them. To look to Christ for eternal salvation means that we abandon all other hopes and depend completely on what Jesus did on the cross.

Finally, as the serpent on the pole was the only way for the people of Israel to be healed, so Christ's death on the cross is the only way God has appointed for our sins to be forgiven.

People mightily object to this in these easy-going, tolerant days. But we must remember again that salvation is God's plan. It doesn't have to suit us. It must suit him. Instead of complaining about the way he has designed, let us be thankful that there is a way and take advantage of it.

41 | The happiness of the people of God

Deuteronomy 33:29

This 33rd chapter of Deuteronomy consists of Moses' farewell address to the people of Israel. After pronouncing blessings upon the various tribes of the nation, Moses moves to his conclusion in which he glories both in God (vv.26-27) and in the happiness of the people of God (v.29). Matthew Henry writes: 'Moses, the man of God...with his last breath magnifies both the God of Israel and the Israel of God. They are both incomparable in his eye; and we are sure that in his judgment of both his eye did not wax dim.'[1]

We are focusing on the last words of Moses' last words, that is, on that part of his conclusion in which he glories in the happiness of the people of God.

Moses could have closed his farewell address in countless ways, but he chose to stress the blessedness of the people of God. He wanted to give them one last reminder of how very blessed they were to have been singled out and made distinct from all the other nations. Sufficiently realizing this would protect them from many dangers and would spur them to live in obedience to the Lord.

We look at this verse because it applies as much to the people of God now as it did on that occasion. And to the extent that we realize our blessedness will we be protected from various snares and inclined to faithfully serve the Lord.

How few of us really appreciate the magnitude of our blessedness! Let's pray that God will help us see more of it as we examine Moses' words.

First, Moses called the people's attention to the blessing of salvation.

He says:

> *Happy are you, O Israel!*
> *Who is like you,*
> *a people saved by the Lord!*

It is true, of course, that the people were 'saved' in a political way when God delivered them from bondage in Egypt. And they were 'saved' in a physical way when God opened the Red Sea before them and when he sustained them time and time again in their wilderness journeys. But those instances of salvation paled in comparison to another type, that is, the spiritual salvation that believing Israelites enjoyed as they looked forward in faith to the coming Messiah.

The very fact that Moses has already made mention of the 'eternal God' as their refuge, the God who has 'everlasting arms' ought to be enough to convince us that he had eternal salvation in mind. In addition to that we have several instances of New Testament writers seeing Israel's political and temporal deliverances as pictures of eternal salvation (1 Cor. 5:7; 10:1-13).

Now there are a couple of things for us to notice about the salvation that Israel enjoyed. First, it was completely the Lord's doing. Moses says they had been 'saved by the Lord.' Secondly, it set them apart from all other nations and peoples. Moses asks: 'Who is like you, …'.

Why are we dealing with all of this? The answer is, of course, that all believers today are saved by exactly the same Lord in exactly the same way (through faith in the Christ) as those to whom Moses spoke in his address.

We have been saved by the Lord! Salvation is not part our doing and part his. It is entirely his. We can take no more credit for it than the Israelites could for their deliverance from Egypt or Jonah could for his deliverance from the fish. God planned our salvation in eternity past. There he chose his people (Eph. 1:3-4). He announced it after Adam and Eve fell into sin. He continually pictured it for the people of the Old Testament. And he finally provided it in the coming, living, dying and rising of his Son, Jesus. Charles Spurgeon says: 'free grace must wear the crown.'[2]

But all this raises a most vital and urgent question, namely, why do we need salvation. There can be no salvation unless there is something to be saved from. Salvation implies extreme, critical danger. Where there is no danger there can be no salvation.

The Bible is very explicit about the nature of our danger. It tells us that we are all by nature sinners, and because of our sins we are under the sentence of the holy God who must judge sin and has pronounced sentence upon it. That sentence is nothing less than his wrath which will finally be manifested in eternal separation from God and all that is lovely and good.

This was our situation. But God has saved us through his Son. By living his perfect life, the Lord Jesus provided the righteousness his people lack. By dying on the cross, he received the wrath they deserve. All who by the grace of God believe in that redeeming work are freed from their sins, adopted into the family of God and given title to eternal glory. What a marvellous thing salvation is!

Charles Spurgeon, as he so often does, gets at something of the marvel in these memorable words: 'Why that one word "saved" is enough to make the heart dance as long as life remains. "Saved!" Let us hang out our banners and set the bells a-ringing. Saved! What a sweet sound it is to the man who is wrecked and sees the vessel going down, but at that moment discovers that the life-boat is near and will rescue him from the sinking ship. To be snatched from devouring fire, or saved from fierce disease, just when the turning point has come, and death appears imminent, these also are occasions for crying, "Saved." But to be rescued from sin and hell is a greater salvation still, and demands a louder joy. We will sing it in life and whisper it in death, and chant it throughout eternity—saved by the Lord.'[3]

Spurgeon also says: ' ... I would fire your hearts with enthusiasm towards him who loved you before the earth was, who, having chosen you, purchased you with a price immense, brought you out from among the rest of mankind by his power, separated you unto himself to be his people for ever, and who loves you with a love that will never weary nor grow cold, but will bring you unto himself and seat you at this right hand for ever and ever, and who now loves you with a love that will never weary nor grow cold, but will bring you unto himself and seat you at his right hand for ever and ever.'[4]

This salvation makes us separate and distinct from all those who have not received it. Only those who have faith in Christ are saved. And what a privilege this is! On the other hand, how very sad and lamentable it is that those of us who claim to be saved often seem to envy the world. We should be the envy of the world and not envy the world. We should live in such a way that those around us will know that we are saved and that being saved is the most wonderful thing in all the world.

Having attributed the happiness of the people to their salvation, Moses proceeded to a second reason for it, that is,

They were shielded by the same Lord

Moses calls the Lord 'the shield' of their help. The Lord had indeed shielded them from all sorts of enemies and dangers, and he would continue to do so as they made their way into the land of Canaan.

God has not stopped his shielding work. The people of God are still surrounded by foes and dangers. The world, the flesh and the devil are still with us. As we contemplate the reality and the strength of these enemies, we can most certainly join John Newton in saying:

> *Thro' many dangers, toils and snares,*
> *I have already come;*
> *'Tis grace hath bro't me safe thus far,*
> *And grace will lead me home.*

After we are saved, we are shielded from Satan. He can never claim us again or enslave us. We are shielded from countless disasters, many of which we are completely unaware. And we will be shielded in the hour of death and safely escorted into the presence of our God. No weapon formed against the people of God can ever prosper or succeed (Isa. 54:17).

Saved and shielded! Happy are the people of God!

If Moses had said no more, we would be able to rejoice forever, but he carried the people to yet another level, namely,

Their triumph through the Lord

Moses calls the Lord 'the sword' of their 'majesty'. In other words, the Lord was the one by whom they would achieve excellency and glory in the land of Canaan which they were about to enter, which, as we have established, can be regarded as a picture of spiritual truth that pertains to us. And what is that spiritual truth? It is that the same God who saved us and shields us will finally raise us to triumphantly share in the excellent glory of heaven, which is our inheritance as much as Canaan was the inheritance of the Israelites.

This is the positive side of what we have just noticed. The people of God, then, are not only shielded from their enemies but will finally be triumphant over them. The same God who keeps us from being hurt by them will destroy them, and, the people of God will share in and rejoice over that triumph.

Child of God, does you heart feel tired and old? Here is good medicine for it – saved! shielded! victorious! Ponder these words until you can say: 'Happy are you, O believer!'

Deuteronomy 34:1-12

Forty years after their departure from Egypt, the people of Israel were finally ready to begin their conquest of the land of Canaan.

It had to be a time of mixed emotions. Tremendous happiness and excitement over the forthcoming conquest mingled with sadness that Moses, their long-time leader, would not be with them.

The time had come for Moses to die. Joseph Hall says of Moses at this time: 'He hath brought his Israelites from Egypt, through the sea and wilderness, within the sight of their promised land: and now himself must take possession of that land, whereof Canaan was but a type.'[1]

Many will go to almost any length to avoid thinking about death, but we do well to think about it. Moses' death will help us to that end. It lays before us certain truths about death that are vital for our consideration.

First, Moses' death serves as a reminder that...

We must all die

Great a man as he was, Moses still had to die. Only Enoch and Elijah have been whisked from this earth without having to experience the pangs of death. The fact that they were the only ones proves the truth of these words: 'it is appointed for men to die' (Heb. 9:27).

The same Bible that is so emphatic about the certainty of death is equally so about this: death is not the end. It is merely the door through which we pass into eternity. And eternity itself is divided into life and death.

With the awesome reality of eternity looming before us, it would seem reasonable for us to make dying the major concern of living. But how many there are who live as if they will never have to die and never have to go into eternity!

We must never forget that Moses died as a child of God, that is, as one who had trusted in the redeeming work that the Messiah would do. If we want to enter the blissful part of eternity as he did, we must have the same faith that he had.

A second truth for us to glean from the death of Moses is this:

The Lord tenderly cares for his people when they die

Moses died 'according to the word of the Lord' (v.5) and with the presence of the Lord. We know this is true because of these words: 'And He buried him in a valley in the land of Moab' (v.6).

Moses had the sovereign God for his undertaker and the mighty angels for his pallbearers.

We cannot fully appreciate this if we do not recall one of the major aspects of Moses' death. It was not because he was old and decrepit. Although he was 120 years old, his 'eyes were not dim nor his natural vigor abated' (v.7).

Moses had to die at this time because he had disobeyed the Lord, and, as a judgement, the Lord had announced that he would not enter the land of Canaan with the people (Num. 20:1-13).

But the fact that Moses had sinned did not sever his relationship with God or negate the Lord's gracious and tender care for him.

When the saint of God approaches death, the minions of hell may very well gather around his deathbed to leer at him and to terrify him with thoughts about his failings.

But the sins of the saints cannot overturn the grace of God. If we were saved by our performance, we would do well to tremble at the thought of our sins. But our redemption is secured, by the performance of the Lord Jesus Christ on our behalf. Let the devil find a flaw with that, and then the saint will tremble. But, thank God, there is no flaw to be found.

Simon Peter denied the Lord Jesus three times. Breathtaking failure! But that failure did not negate the grace of God, and John 21 shows Jesus in full pursuit of his deeply flawed disciple.

David failed miserably. Adultery, murder, deception! What a list! But David found forgiveness (Ps. 32), and when he came to the end of life's journey, he also found the Lord there in the valley of the shadow of death (Ps. 23:4).

His sins, large as they were, were not large enough to drive the Lord away. Charles Spurgeon was right to say: 'Ah, the bridge of grace will bear your weight, brother. Thousands of big sinners have gone across that bridge, yea, tens of thousands have gone over it. ... and yet never a stone has sprung in that mighty bridge.'[2]

The God whom we offend when we sin does not hate us because of our sins. He sees us clothed in the righteousness of his Son, and he loves us with an everlasting love that cannot be toppled by our sins.

Loving us as he does, he rushes to meet us in the hour of death so that he can receive us unto himself, completely rid us of every vestige of sin and enter into eternal fellowship with us.

What a wonderful God we have!

What does the Lord do to help his dying people other than grant them his presence? He shows them the land of promise. While Moses was not permitted to enter the land of Canaan, the Lord did give him a grand view of it (vv.1-4).

Joseph Hall draws this consoling conclusion: 'It is the goodness of our God, that he will not have his children die any where, but where they may see the land of promise before them'[3]

There is no tour guide like God!

Moses' death calls us to consider a third truth:

We die best if we have faithfully served the Lord

This truth is placed before us by these words: 'So Moses the servant of the Lord died...' (v.5).

Isn't it interesting that Moses is not called the leader of Israel or the deliverer of Israel or the law-giver of Israel? He is merely called the servant of the Lord.

We have rejoiced over the truth that the Lord's grace is certainly greater than all our sins. We must not allow that knowledge to make us careless about sin. We should rather seek to live in such a way that we will have as few regrets as possible when we die. And the fewness of our regrets will be in direct proportion to the faithfulness of our service.

Much these days is made of mastering leadership principles. We should all be more concerned about mastering servanthood principles. We will die better if we do.

Charles Spurgeon pointedly calls us to serve the Lord in these words: 'As long as there is breath in our bodies, let us serve Christ. As long as we can think, as long as we can speak, as long as we can work, let us serve him. Let us even serve him with our last gasp. And, if it be possible, let us try to set some work going that will glorify him when we are dead and gone. Let us scatter some seed that may spring up when we are sleeping beneath the hillock in the cemetery.'[4]

Let's look to Moses' death for yet another lesson:

The Lord's work goes on

We read these words: 'So Moses the servant of the Lord died...' (v.5).

A little later we read: 'Now Joshua the son of Nun was full of the spirit of wisdom, for Moses had laid his hands on him; so the children of Israel heeded him, and did as the Lord had commanded Moses' (v.9).

It could very well be that many Israelites vexed themselves over the future when Moses died. What would become of them now? Would Joshua be up to the challenge?

If they were anxious about the matter, it was because they failed to see that the reason for Israel's success and the guarantee of her future was not Moses but God. The Lord did not die with Moses! And the same God who was sufficient for him would be sufficient for Joshua. No one is irreplaceable in the work of the Lord.

Let us always be thankful for the ministries of good men, but let us never give the praise to those men that belongs to the God who sent them.

Let us also learn not to despair over the work of the Lord. It often appears that the cause of God is going to fail, but it will not. The Lord will preserve his cause now even as he did when Moses died. The gates of hell will not prevail against the church (Matt. 16:18).

43 | The prophet like Moses

Deuteronomy 18:15-18

The book of Deuteronomy is primarily Moses preaching. It begins with this statement: 'These are the words which Moses spoke' (1:1).

The book proceeds to present three of Moses' sermons (1:5-4:43; 4:44-28:68; 29:1-31:29). It closes with the song of Moses (31:30-32:43), his final blessing (32:44-33:29) and the account of his death (34:1-12), which may very well have been written by Joshua.

It is not the least bit surprising that we have all these words from Moses. Before he took his leave of the people and before they began their conquest of the land of Canaan, it is only to be expected that he would remind them of the laws of God (Deuteronomy means 'second law') and work out for them both the implications of obedience and disobedience.

In the midst of his very long second sermon (4:44-28:68), Moses offered a cheering prediction: 'The Lord your God will raise up for you a Prophet like me from your midst, from your brethren' (v.15).

This was not just wishful thinking on Moses' part. It was not just a piece of 'pie in the sky' optimism. It was rather Moses accurately declaring what God had said to him (vv.17-22),

To whom was Moses referring? Who is the prophet about whom he prophesied? It is clear that the Jews did not consider this prophecy to have been fulfilled when Jesus came. However, many did regard Jesus as its fulfilment (John 6:14).

No one before Jesus fulfilled the prophecy, and no one since could possibly fulfil it (Heb. 1:1-2). The prophet to whom Moses referred, then, was none other than Jesus himself.

As we have worked our way through the life of Moses, we have frequently reminded ourselves of his role as mediator. Moses, of course, could only faintly foreshadow the true mediator – the Lord Jesus.

A mediator is a 'go-between.' He comes between parties in conflict and makes peace. Jesus came to make peace between the holy God and sinful people. This work of mediation required Jesus to fill three roles, namely, prophet, priest and king. Our salvation hinges on him serving in these capacities and doing so in a flawless way.

As priest, Jesus made peace by offering himself as the sacrifice for sinners. As king, Jesus makes peace by ruling in the hearts of his people.

And as prophet, Jesus makes peace by faithfully proclaiming the truth of God. There can be no peace between God and sinners until the latter are willing to hear the truth of God and to submit to it. This is essential because one of the primary results of sin is that our minds are darkened (1 Cor. 2:14; 2 Cor. 4:4).

The words of Moses about Jesus the Prophet give us three major truths to consider.

He was sent by God

Moses stated this truth in these words: 'The Lord your God will raise up for you a Prophet … ' (v.15).

As we have noted, Jesus was that Prophet. Jesus, therefore, was raised up by God. Jesus himself emphasized this throughout his public ministry. He came from God (John 3:16-17; 5:24,30,36-38;6:44,57;7:16;8:16 ,18;9:4;10:36;11:42;12:45,49;14:24;15:21;16:5) to speak for God (John 8:38;14:10,24).

The words Jesus spoke were the words of God himself! What Jesus had to say about the sinful nature of the human heart (Matt. 15:18-19), the certainty of divine judgment (John 5:22-30) and the terrible reality of hell (Matt. 23:33; Mark 9:42-48; Luke 16:19-31) is not merely another man sharing his opinions. It is nothing less than a divine message. And what Jesus had to say about eternal salvation through his own death on the cross is also divine (John 6:47-58).

We are living in days in which many people casually dismiss these truths. Others mightily resent and resist them. Little do they realize that these are divine in nature. Men could not come to them if they would and would not come to them if they could.

Because these truths are divine they are certain and imperishable. We can deny them, despise them and dispute them, but we cannot destroy them. The course of wisdom, then, is to both recognize that Jesus spoke the words of God and humbly submit to them. It is to do nothing less than heed the words of Moses himself: 'Him you shall hear' (v.15).

The course of wisdom is to heed this word of warning from the Lord himself: 'And it shall be that whoever will not hear My word, which He speaks in My name, I will require it of him' (v.18).

The Pharisees of Jesus' day refused to heed his words. To them Jesus said: 'He who is of God hears God's words; therefore you do not hear, because you are not of God' (John 8:47).

He was like Moses

The Prophet whom God promised to send would be like Moses (v.15).

What kind of prophet was Moses? The author of Hebrews supplies the answer. He tells us that Moses was a faithful servant in God's house, and the Lord Jesus is worthy of even more glory because he is the Son over the house (Heb. 3:1-6).

Jesus was 'like Moses' in faithfulness. But he also surpassed Moses in this respect and in every other. Moses was not perfect in faithfulness (Num. 20:1-13), but Jesus was. As God's Prophet, Jesus never failed to accurately declare the Word of God and never failed to live up to that word which he declared.

Is this important? Our salvation depends on it! If Jesus had not been faithful to God in every respect, he would have been a sinner himself and would have had to pay for his own sins. If he would have had sins of his own, he could not have paid for the sins of others. That's how very important it is!

He was from the people

In keeping with what the Lord had revealed to him (v.18), Moses affirmed that the Prophet would arise 'from your midst, from your brethren' (v.15).

When the people of Israel were gathered at Mt. Sinai, the Lord spoke to them directly from heaven with thunder clapping, lightning streaking and smoke bellowing (Exod. 20:18-19).

Matthew Henry says: 'Every word made their ears tingle and their hearts tremble, so that the whole congregation was ready to die with fear. In this fright, they begged hard that God would not speak to them in this manner any more ... but that he would speak to them by men like themselves, by Moses now, and afterwards by other prophets like unto him.... Thus, in answer to the request of those who were struck with amazement by the law, God promised the incarnation of his Son.'[1]

We must not think, however, that God had never conceived of the incarnation before this. The request of the people simply gave him the opportunity to declare once more what he planned from eternity and announced several times before.

We have established that the prophetic office Jesus came to discharge was mediatorial in nature. He came between the holy God and sinners to make peace. In this role, it was essential for him to be able to fully represent both parties.

Since he was already God, there was no difficulty in him representing God. In order to represent human beings he had to be one. Here is the wonder and glory of the incarnation: Jesus added to his deity our humanity so that he was at one and the same time fully God and fully man.

He could not have done anything for us had he not been one of us. The author of Hebrews says of Christ: 'Inasmuch then as the children have partaken of flesh and blood, He Himself likewise shared in the same, ... ' (Heb. 2:14).

He then proceeds to say: 'For indeed He does not give aid to angels, but He does give aid to the seed of Abraham. Therefore, in all things He had to be made like His brethren, that He might be a merciful and faithful High Priest in things pertaining to God, to make propitiation for the sins of the people' (Heb. 2:16-17).

While the author wrote these words in connection with the priestly office of Christ, they certainly apply to the prophetic role he came to discharge.

How gracious it was of God to send his Son to take up our humanity and in that humanity to speak to us the words of eternal life! We do not realize and appreciate to a sufficient degree what God has done to provide salvation for us.

Sent by God! Faithful like Moses! Sent as one of us! What a prophet we have in Jesus! How we should prize his prophetic work! And we prize him in that role only if we do as Moses said, that is, hear him.

It is significant that this section closes with a warning about false prophets (vv.19-22). Because Jesus was the Prophet, we should have no trouble discerning them. Anyone who denies the truth Jesus taught, denies him, and anyone who denies Jesus is dead wrong.

Notes

Chapter 1 – The world into which Moses was born
[1] John Currid, *Exodus*, Evangelical Press, pp.46-7.

Chapter 3 – Behind the scenes
[1] Matthew Henry, *Matthew Henry's Commentary on the Whole Bible*,
Fleming H. Revell Company, vol.ii, p.1121.

Chapter 4 – Moses turns his back
[1] J.C. Ryle, *Holiness*, p.136.
[2] As above.
[3] Elisabeth Elliot, *Through Gates of Splendor*, Crossings Classics, title page.

Chapter 5 – The university
[1] Henry Law, *The Gospel in Exodus*, The Banner of Truth Trust, pp.9-10.

Chapter 6 – Please excuse me!
[1] Michael Bentley, *Travelling Homeward*, Evangelical Press, p.69.

Chapter 7 – Moses runs into trouble
[1] William Kirk Kilpatrick, *Psychological Seduction*, Thomas Nelson
Publishers, p.165.

Chapter 10 – Good things to know
[1] Cited by Charles Spurgeon in *Metropolitan Tabernacle Pulpit*, Pilgrim
Publications, Pasadena, Texas, 1983, vol.xvi, p.707.

Chapter 11 – The crossing of the Red Sea
[1] Jonathan Edwards, *The Works of Jonathan Edwards*, The Banner of
Truth Trust, vol.i, p.546.

Chapter 12 – Three songs of praise
[1] Henry, *Commentary*, vol.i, p.337.
[2] Geoffrey B. Wilson, *Revelation*, Evangelical Press, p.127.
[3] Richard Brooks, *The Lamb is all the Glory*, Evangelical Press, p.145.

Chapter 13 – When you arrive at Marah
[1] Bentley, *Travelling Homeward*, p.191.
[2] S.G. DeGraaf, *Promise and Deliverance*, Paideia Press, vol.i, p.287.

Chapter 14 – Manna from heaven
[1] Law, *The Gospel in Exodus*, p.59.
[2] As above.

Chapter 15 – God's provision
[1] Cited by Henry T. Mahan in *With New Testament Eyes: Genesis to Job*, Evangelical Press, p.50.

Chapter 16 – Lessons for spiritual warfare
[1] Law, *The Gospel in Exodus*, p.71.
[2] As above.
[3] As above.
[4] As above, p.72.

Chapter 19 – The Ten Commandments
[1] A.W. Pink, *The Doctrine of Salvation*, Baker Book House, p.49.
[2] Cited by Bentley, *Travelling Homeward*, p.225.

Chapter 20 – The tabernacle
[1] A.W. Pink, *Gleanings in Exodus*, Moody Press, p.204.

Chapter 21- Present truths
[1] Bentley, *Travelling*, p.289.
[2] Henry, *Commentary*, vol.i, p.394.
[3] As above.

Chapter 22 – The golden calf
[1] Michael Horton, *In the Face of God*, Word Publishing, p.21.

Chapter 23 – The tent of meeting
[1] D. Martyn Lloyd-Jones, *Revival*, Crossway Books, p.163.

Chapter 24 – Moses in prayer
[1] Law, *The Gospel in Exodus*, p.152.
[2] Alexander Maclaren, *Expositions of Holy Scripture*, Baker Book House, vol.i, p.191.
[3] As above, p.192.
[4] As above.
[5] Law, *The Gospel in Exodus*, p.152.

Chapter 25 – God proclaims his name
[1] Law, *The Gospel in Exodus*, p.153.
[2] As above.
[3] As above, p.154.
[4] As above, p.157.

Chapter 26 – The glory of Moses
[1] Maclaren, *Expositions*, vol.i, p.208.
[2] Charles R. Erdman, *The Gospel of Matthew*, The Westminster Press, p.136.

Chapter 27 – Will you not come and join us?
[1] Edward D. Griffin, *The Life and Sermons of Edward D. Griffin*, The Banner of Truth Trust, vol.i, pp.574-5.

Chapter 28 – Losing sight of the calling
[1] DeGraaf, *Promise and Deliverance*, vol.i, p.333.
[2] As above, pp.335-6.

Chapter 29 – Questions for the journey
[1] DeGraaf, *Promise and Deliverance*, vol.i, p.337.
[2] Henry, *Commentary*, vol.i, p.613.

Chapter 30 – Journey to jealousy
[1] Joseph Hall, *Hall's Contemplations*, Soli Deo Gloria Publications, vol.i, p.178.
[2] As above, p.179.

[1] DeGraaf, *Promise and Deliverance*, vol.i, p.343.
[2] Hall, *Contemplations*, vol.i, p.182.

Chapter 32 – Three prayings
[1] John Gill, *Expositions of the Old & New Testaments*, The Baptist Standard Bearer, Inc., vol.i, p.770.
[2] Maclaren, *Expositions*, vol.i, p.352.

Chapter 35 – Modern lessons
[1] Cited by R.T. Kendall, *The Westminster Record*, Westminster Chapel, April, 1980, vol.55, no.4, p.238.
[2] Henry, *Commentary*, vol.i,p.637.
[3] As above.
[4] As above, p.638.

Chapter 36 – A day of reckoning
[1] DeGraaf, *Promise and Deliverance*, vol.i, p.353.
[2] As above.

Chapter 37 – An old picture
[1] Gordon Keddie, *According to Promise*, Evangelical Press, pp.118-9.
[2] Mahan, *With New Testament Eyes*, p.66.
[3] Hall, *Contemplations*, vol.i, p.194.
[4] Keddie, *According to Promise*, p.121.
[5] Mahan, *With New Testament Eyes*, p.68.

Chapter 38 – Encouragement from a stick
[1] Walter Chantry, *Praises for the King of Kings*, The Banner of Truth Trust, p.110.

Chapter 39 – What God takes seriously
[1] Keddie, *According to Promise*, p.142.
[2] Pink, *Gleanings in Exodus*, p.139.

Chapter 41 – The happiness of the people of God
[1] Henry, *Commentary*, vol.i, p.882.
[2] Spurgeon, *Metropolitan Tabernacle Pulpit*, vol.xxiii, p.343.
[3] As above, pp.343-4.